EQUAL PARTNERS

The art of creative marriage

by
Frieda Porat, Ph.D.
and
Jacquelyn Carr, Ph.D.

R&E PUBLISHERS
Saratoga, California 95070

Published by
R&E PUBLISHERS
P. O. Box 2008
Saratoga, California 95070

Typesetting by
Estella M. Krebs

Graphics by
Kaye Graphics

Library of Congress Card Catalog Number
86-82249

I.S.B.N.
0-88247-761-7

Library of Congress Cataloging-in-Publication Data

Porat, Frieda, 1925–
   Equal partners.

   Bibliography: p.
   1. Marriage--United States. 2. Interpersonal
relations. 3. Love. I. Carr, Jacquelyn B., 1923–
II. Title.
HQ734.P768 1987   646.7'8   86-82249
ISBN 0-88247-761-7

TO

Sandie and Marc

Ruth and Anthony

and Naomi

—F.P.

Table of Contents

Introduction

We invite you to take a journey, to observe and participate in one of the most complex, meaningful, and fulfilling adventures in your life — the marriage partnership of equals.

Many books have been written on the challenging topic of marriage, so why did we write another one? And more importantly, why should you read another one?

This book is written for people who want to move out of the past and into today on their way to tomorrow, people flexible enough to be on the cutting edge of change, people who are striving for more success in every area of life.

These are exciting times of transformation as new roles emerge for both men and women. It is also a time of stress, disappointment, and struggle. These are times when you and your partner need to support each other more than ever before as you learn to combine your career with marriage and family.

Today the two paycheck marriage is a reality for a large percentage of the population. While men try to cope with working wives, they learn that women do not find fulfillment in simply bringing home a paycheck.

Today women want meaning and purpose in their careers. In giving a new energy and commitment to their jobs, they sometimes bring more stress and anxiety home. They want the love and nurturing support they once gave to their men.

The *new marriage* is a partnership of equals who share similar goals and values, and who support each other's professional ambitions. Success in this new partnership requires you to balance career goals with family issues such as creating quality time for spouses and children.

In helping you create the equal partnership, we explore the myths of marriage that can destroy relationships. We explore the elements of a healthy, vital marriage. We show you how to give your partner nurturing love and respect as equals.

You can learn how to reach beyond the symbiotic relationship that inhibits growth and stifles individuality. In an "Equal Partnership" you will find both autonomy and closeness.

In this book, you will learn how to:

- listen effectively and respond authentically to each other
- set goals as individuals and professionals
- create and sustain excitement and enthusiasm
- use a marriage checkup to renew your commitment
- review and update your marriage contract
- learn how to be lovers over and over again

As you learn to use the suggestions in this book in the process of revitalization, we hope to invoke your curiosity and give you some insight into balancing work and love — the essential elements of life.

We are optimistic about the future of marriage. We encourage you to examine the factors that contribute to a successful marriage, a fulfilling career, and a happy life.

1 Marriage Styles: Past and Present

Nothing endures but change.
Heraclitus

Our world is in transition, moving in directions that will ultimately result in new values and new models. The changes are so pervasive and so complex that we often lose awareness of them. New discoveries demand that we change our views of nature, evolution, progress, time, and space.

No matter where you live – on a farm, in the suburbs, in the city – high technology has pervaded every aspect of your life – agriculture, telecommunications, transportation. Biotech firms are cultivating a better tomato. Even your car and telephone have been transformed with computers that you can't see.

Technology affects business, industry, and science. You may not think that the United States' exploration in space affects you, but it does. When you go to your doctor for an ordinary physical, he has machines that can analyze your pulse rate and respiration to provide a quick assessment of the elasticity of your heart muscle. He can scan your bones to measure their density. Surgeons can perform operations without surgery.

Because of technology, we are living longer. Every aspect of our lives is affected including our economic lives. Many women have gone to work. Life in this High-Tech world, with all its changes, affects how we human beings relate to one another.

What about our values? According to a national survey, having a happy marriage outranks a successful career. Asked to rank the importance of a happy marriage as part of "the good life," on a 100-point scale, women rated it 90, men 88. A successful career was

1

rated 82 by women, 81 by men. Although each of us can choose the kind of life we want to live, we need to know what we want and how much a good life costs. We can learn to balance love, work, and leisure for a good life.

Most Americans believe that a stable marriage is the best way to live. We talk about a *successful* marriage, but hesitate to define the words. Most definitions come from our culture, our parents, and grandparents. However, our culture is rapidly changing. American values seem to be in a constant state of flux. Therefore, it is essential that each of you develops your own definitions of a good life.

Traditionally, a woman married for economic reasons, while a man married to get a housekeeper and children who would work and support him in his old age. Although those traditional reasons still affect us, most Americans today believe a successful marriage includes friendship, affection, and lasting love.

The Fifties

In the 1950's a successful marriage, according to the Puritan ethic, was a sacred institution. Most people of childbearing years (96 percent) married and believed their marriage would last forever. Monogamy was expected. Roles of husband and wife were clearly defined — the woman's place was in the home, and the man was the breadwinner.

Stability and security went hand in hand with marriage. The Golden Wedding Anniversary symbolized the ideal goal. A marriage was defined as successful if the man and wife stayed together until one of them died.

In the 50's, many married people believed that "Love would conquer all." They believed that if a couple were sexually attracted to each other, sex would solve other problems in the marriage. Some believed that marriage should be totally harmonious and without conflict. They also believed in "Togetherness" and spent all their leisure time together. The myths — sex solves other problems, marriage should be without conflict, togetherness brings happiness — often led to disillusionment, resentment, and unhappiness.

The Sixties and Seventies

In the 1960's, the post-war baby boomers came of age. They rebelled against their parents' values. In ten years, the annual per capita income increased from $1595 to $2450. Affluence brought restlessness and freedom marches.

2

A successful marriage became an "open marriage" where each partner was free to do "his or her own thing." Experiments with group marriages and communes lasted from a few months to a decade. The Growth Movement, with its multiple kinds of experimental marriages, represented a rebellion against old values. Freedom and independence, as values, replaced togetherness and commitment. Toward the end of the sixties, one primary movement called "Zero Population Control" resulted in a birthrate drop.

In the *seventies*, the Human Potential Movement, with its emphasis on experimentation, freedom, and multiple options, flourished. Values such as loyalty, monogamy, and permanence — previously accepted for generations — were challenged. One popular slogan of "The Me Generation" became, "You do your thing and I'll do mine." Over time, many couples found some of these attitudes didn't work in a marriage.

Moving Into the Eighties

As the national government went through a period of undisciplined spending and debt, more women moved into the work force. They found that two income families not only have more money but more complicated lives. Married couples decided to have fewer children if they had them at all.

Recently, researchers have found a direct connection between divorce rates and the economy. In times of depression, there are fewer divorces. During times of affluence, divorce rates soar. However, affluence provides us with only one small piece to the complex puzzle which has resulted in today's divorce rate.

A hundred years ago, there was one divorce for every 1,234 marriages. At the turn of the century, when the lifespan was only 49 years, there was one divorce for every 500 marriages. By 1920, there was one divorce for every 12 marriages; and by 1940, one per 6 marriages. Today, 1 out of 2 marriages ends in divorce.

Yet, far from being discouraged, Americans believe so much in marriage that seventy-five percent of divorced people remarry within five years. Of these, 65 percent divorce again. By 1990, statisticians predict more people will be in second marriages than first ones.

To define a successful marriage simply by length of time or on endurance without consideration for quality in the marital relationship is naive.

Although many marriages ended during the sixties and seventies, others survived. Today, people are again reviewing their values.

3

They are taking a hard look at marriage as a realistic choice rather than as an ideal fantasy. Many people getting married today have found that the values of the 1960's and '70's didn't work. Now they want to return to the more conventional values of the past — loyalty, trust, commitment, permanence. They are reconfirming the value of marriage.

For the first time, many Americans are *choosing* marriage as a lifestyle. Without illusions, they know marriage is riskier, more interesting, and more challenging today than at any other time in history. Ultimately, although living as a single person is an option, most people believe marriage can lead to more fulfillment in life.

Those who are married must constantly redefine their marriage. Many couples have learned, from negative experiences, that they do *not* want a traditional marriage. They want to revise the rules of marriage.

After making the decision that their marriage is worth keeping and that they want to stay married to each other, many married couples are renewing their commitments at a deeper level. They want to know how to make new kinds of agreements, how to keep communication open, and how to resolve conflicts.

Many young people today are postponing marriage and children to pursue education and careers. Because fewer Americans are getting married and fewer are staying married, those who do marry have a better chance at success. They can expect to forge better relationships. The decline in marriages and number of children per married pair signals a new American family in the making.

The women's movement and the sexual revolution have transformed the way Americans decide on marriage. As more women work outside the home, fewer feel financially dependent on men. No longer do women believe they have to get married in order to be supported. Sexual freedom and reliable contraception allow both sexes to look over potential mates carefully before committing to marriage. The American family as we have known it is changing. Similarly, what is considered a suitable marital relationship is changing.

Working women who are married want men to share equally in child-raising and household tasks. Although men often say they are willing to do their share, their actions do not yet live up to their words.

Most working women surveyed today say they do "double duty." For example, a famous woman television personality who recently had twins says that her famous writer husband will help with the babies, but he waits until she tells him when they must be

4

changed and when they must be fed. In effect, she is the responsible party.

Even though salaries for women increase family income, women still take on most of the responsibilities connected with child care and running the house. As a result, young married wives who work often fight resentment, guilt, and conflict.

The ideal of a fifty-fifty marriage has yet to be translated into practice. Many women are not ready to give up their roles as fulltime caretakers of the house and family. Traditionally, wives have taken responsibility for family health and nutrition.

Women don't easily ask their mates for help. They expect themselves to be able to handle "it all" — the house, the nutrition and health needs, the children. By asking for assistance, they are afraid they will admit failure, antagonize or frighten their families, or make themselves feel guilty. In effect, women want to see themselves as strong, independent and self-sufficient by "doing it all."

Men are more work-centered. Although they may not be aware of it, men are afraid something serious might happen to the women they depend upon and love. Men are no longer consistently the authority figures in the household. They allow their women to protect the household domain. They are confused by the demand for a 50-50 division of the work when, in fact, how they do it often meets with irritation or disapproval.

Men have not been taught nor are they expected to nurture their partners. They have few role models to follow. In this cultural transition, women must teach their men how to satisfy nurturing needs.

The new *high-tech* marriage is moving slowly toward autonomy and equality. These changes, now in transition, often cause confusion or conflict because we are not fully aware of what is happening to us.

To many people, these changes from the 1950's seem to represent a "breakdown" in the family. However, the 1890 census figures on marriage are similar to today's. In both 1890 and 1980, men and women are waiting longer to get married — if they decide to get married at all. Therefore, the 1950's, when 96 percent of adults married, was atypical rather than the norm. As a result, the entire structure of what we have come to think of as the typical family is now in transition.

Many marriages move in the fast lane. Dual career couples want equality and emotional support from each other in both success and failure. They also want quality time together to make such joint decisions as whether to have children or live without children.

If either or both parties are in a second marriage, they may have

5

to consider ex-spouses, ex-in-laws, blended families, and the resolution of past issues. Parents must consider separation anxieties experienced by children who may feel abandoned after a divorce. Couples must adjust to step-parent roles and extended family relationships. They must live with new routines and develop new rituals. But, most difficult of all, they must learn to trust and love again.

New, extended families include his children, her children, and their children. All of these new family forms make up today's reality. Couples who make the commitment to permanence want to learn ways to make their marriages work.

When a large sample of brilliant, successful men and women were asked to look back on their lives to what was most satisfying, the vast majority said their families had been the most fulfilling and satisfying part of their lives in spite of their accomplishments, status, and financial success. Marriage and family have been and will continue to be high on the American list of values.

To be married today means to choose marriage. Individuals with a strong sense of self and a developed self-esteem can reconfirm the value of marriage. After the historical experiences of the last twenty years, most couples today value monogamy, loyalty, and commitment.

A successful marriage is defined as one in which two people respect and like each other, become friends, agree on mutual values and goals, and make marriage a lifetime contract. They want to make the relationship succeed and are willing to work together to solve problems. They expect to find satisfaction and fulfillment together. A successful marriage combines quality in a relationship with stability.

Today's Options

The main issue for two-career couples is how to be successful in the various functions of job, marriage, and parenthood. Traditionally, men tried to be superior in their work as an extension of their masculinity. Being aggressive on the job, being competitive in climbing the ladder to success, and becoming affluent fit society's standards for a successful mate.

Traditionally, women tried to be superior as wives and mothers which was an extension of their feminity. Being submissive, non-assertive, and dependent financially fit society's image of a successful female.

The successful married couple, consequently, was the professional male with a supportive wife who, in addition to maintaining the house and family, supported her husband in fulfilling his goals. She socialized with the key people in her husband's business, made friends with their wives, and entertained according to his position and professional needs. Such women did not expect recognition for their contributions to their husbands' successes.

Today, as women have become more equal to men in their ambitions to succeed on the job, they are making a commitment to excellence and leadership in the work world. This kind of commitment takes time, effort, and energy — almost a single-focused attention to work.

As a result, the choices are many. Some women have decided to stay single. Others have combined work and marriage, but have decided not to have children. Some women have decided to delay starting their families until they have achieved some success in their career while carefully watching their biological "clocks." Some women have decided to have only one child which they believe will not interfere with their career goals. Other women either have children before they begin their careers or believe they can combine children and work.

Most women who have attempted to divide themselves emotionally among three roles — work, wife, parent — have discovered that being excellent in all three can exact a high price. Their work suffers, or their marriages fail, or their children are neglected. No woman can be a "super-professional," a "super-wife," and a "super-mom" over a long period of time without suffering physically or emotionally. If she ignores herself as a human being and fails to nurture herself, the consequence can be great.

In the past, men were able to place their work first. Their wives accepted long absences, travel, evening work, as coming before the marriage and family. However, this superficial acceptance by wives resulted in deep feelings of resentment and abandonment. These feelings often led to a breakdown in communication, mutual withdrawal, or dissolution of the marriage.

As a result of the women's movement, women moved into the work force and developed the male qualities of aggressiveness, and competitiveness. Women developed a need to win, to succeed, and to make money. The social rules changed.

Men are now expected to encourage and support their wives in fulfilling educational and professional goals. Men, today, are asked to do housework and take care of children. Although many men verbally accept this transition, covertly they resist housework and childcare by taking a secondary role. Often passive resistance takes the form of, "I forgot," "What should I do?", "I don't know how to do that," "You do it better."

This passive-aggression, "under-dog" role is a form of sabotage. One woman says,

"Yes, my husband will change a diaper when I tell him the baby needs to be changed. He will feed the baby if I tell him it is time. But then he asks me what the baby eats and where is it. If I have to tell him when, what and how, I'd rather do it myself. But then I'm angry."

Such negative feelings teach women they cannot be excellent in all three roles — work, wife, and mother — without the help of a supportive husband. The entire family must agree on the price they are willing to pay for a modern marriage. When these conflicts are communicated, negotiated, and resolved; superior marriages can be created.

Some young men brought up with the social rules of the last twenty years have given up the stereotypical masculine image. They are more apt to see women and men as human beings with similar needs and goals. They not only participate in the marriage and child-rearing but also take the initiative in determining the direction of the marriage and family. They take an active interest in nurturing their marriage, wife, and children.

The satisfactions they experience in quality relationships with their wives and children often replace their ambitions in the work world. They have given up the driving, striving, money-making rat race.

These new men do *not* want to be #1. The cost is too great. At the end of an eight-hour-day, they want to go home. Fulfillment, for them, is reached through a balance of work, marriage and family.

In the fifties, the primary pattern was a successful husband who divorced his wife, and gave her the house, children, alimony, and child support. He had visitation rights and joint custody, but he tended to remarry and leave his past. Women and children felt abandoned. They rarely had any voice in such decisions.

In the eighties, successfully married couples, being realistic, expect to have problems, not all of which can be solved. They learn that crises are an important element within marriage. They decide not to allow a crisis to end in divorce or in a deadly war of endurance. A crisis can be a growing experience.

How To Get the Most Out of This Book

It's not enough just to read about the changes going on around you. You wouldn't expect to be able to play the piano after reading a book about it, so you mustn't expect your marriage to change because you read a book about marriage. We suggest you start a notebook, right now! Review this chapter looking for thoughts, ideas, insights that you find valuable. Jot down questions, feelings, conclusions that are your personal responses to what is here.

Divide the notebook into sections based on the chapters in this book. Then devise whatever system you want that reenforces your commitment to write. Like making New Year's resolutions, we tend to slip back to old behavior patterns. If you do not continue to write, do not feel guilty. You can go back and re-read, as well as write, whenever you want some suggestions about how to make your marriage better.

Begin by answering the following questions:

Issues of Balance
1. What are the most important things in my life?
2. How can I order these in terms of priority?
3. How can I create a balance between self and other?
4. Can I delay some items?
5. Can I be flexible and change sequence?
6. What price am I willing to pay?
7. What kinds of jobs are compatible with family life?
8. Can I and my mate collaborate? Compromise?
9. What stage of life or passage am I experiencing?
10. What items are non-negotiable?
11. What trade-offs am I willing to make? (For example — take turns working, part-time work, self-employment, flex-time, a shared job, etc.)

Through conflict resolution and compromise, through renegotiating their marriage vows with new contracts, through loyalty, monogamy, and renewed commitment; the successfully married couple can expect to reach new plateaus of affection and love. They can expect marriage to remain rich and vital for their entire lives.

Marriage is *not* a myth. Marriage is an expression of intimacy, security, companionship, and love. It begins with two people falling in love, committing themselves to sharing a life with each other, and then finding ways to live out that commitment.

9

2 Marriage Styles: The Myths and Realities of Marriage

Whether you have a problem in your marriage, or you want to learn skills to prevent future problems, or you have a good marriage that you would like to enrich, it's important to examine your options.

- What is your present marriage style?
- Would you like to develop a different style?
- What are the available marriage styles?

Here is a brief overview of various marriage styles as described in *Changing Your Life Style*:

The "Fulfilled" Marriage

This marriage relationship fits all the conventional expectations for a marriage, but it is a myth because it is impossible. The myth of the *fulfilled* marriage presumes that two people can satisfy all the needs and expectations of the other, and by doing so they will be happy forever. The concept of the fulfilled marriage further implies that the very fact that each partner should and will be able to fulfill the other partner's needs makes for happiness. Paradoxically, it does not.

You may be shocked and disappointed by the notion that a fulfilled marriage is impossible because most people interpret this as being completely satisfied all of the time. If you consider this for a moment, you will realize that a constant state of satisfaction, or satiation, itself could become monotonous and, therefore, unsatis-

11

fying.

Be assured, there can be many *moments* of fulfillment within a marriage relationship, just as there are moments of excitement, humor, pain, and discontent. However, being fulfilled does not last. It is a momentary peak experience and people spend more time working toward moments of fulfillment, anticipating the richness of those moments, and then later savoring the memory, than they spend actually being fulfilled.

An obvious example is the sexual orgasm, which lasts only a few moments, but is accompanied by much longer periods of loving, caressing, and even anticipating the hour of making love. If we were able to live all of our lives in the midst of peak experience (which in essence is what we're talking about in the myth of the fulfilled marriage), then it would become monotony rather than peak experience.

A marriage in which each partner continually satisfied every need of the other — even if it were possible — would become stultifying. Still, some couples try for it. This type of marriage, based upon the myth of "two becoming one," is inhibiting, limiting, enforced togetherness. It is marked by fixed and rigid role assignments. Each partner possesses the other and this exclusive "Ownership" limits each partner's development. The fulfilled traditional marriage often sets up an unequal status between man and woman with the woman coming out on the short end. There is a lack of personal freedom which eventually leads to boredom because stimuli from the outside are shut out or limited.

If we see our life within a marriage as a complete world of *you* and *me*, then *us* is the union. In a fulfilled marriage, the union looks like this:

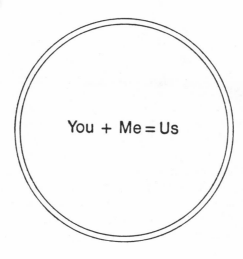

You + Me = Us

The two circles of *you* as an entity and *me* as an entity overlay each other completely. In this togetherness (another word, like fulfilled, which sounds good at first), there is no room for reaching out, for admitting that there are times and places when and where you need separateness. Neither partner acknowledges the freedom to disagree, to be sad, to be you. You may be stifled, swallowed, and drowned by this togetherness. In a fulfilled marriage, you:

1. deny your right to be yourself;
2. own and possess each other;
3. live a life of pretense that you are a quasi-god to each other, and as such you have the ability to fulfill *all* of each other's needs *all* of the time;
4. don't question your roles because that's the way it was and that's the way it will remain.

Fulfilled marriage offers the illusion of security, but it stunts the growth of individuals. In this type of marriage, your dependency upon each other is created by manipulation. The husband in a fulfilled marriage depends upon his wife to provide all the traditional feminine services (creature comforts); the wife depends upon the husband to give her security, and to make her feel needed. The woman is expected to be passive and obedient (the traditional female role), while the man is expected to be authoritarian and controlling (the traditional male role). Even in the most loving and tender relationships, these stereotyped roles and their interaction between man and woman can lead to utter boredom and frustration.

The Limited Partnership

Another option in marriage is the *limited partnership*.

Are you confused by the word partnership? Does the word sound too businesslike, cold, and impersonal for application to a marriage? Let's look at what we mean by a partnership.

A partnership can be defined as a commitment between interested parties to join together in a venture in which everyone gains. A business partnership is set up primarily for monetary gain. In a marriage partnership, the gain may be partially material, but emotional as well. The more effective the partnership, the more gain both parties will receive; therefore, the more incentive they will have to stay in it and renew it.

If the gains are unlimited, why do we define this category of marriage as a limited partnership?

The nature of the limited partnership is that both partners *realize* and *accept* the fact that their partner has limitations. They also recognize that they have limited power to change each other. If your partner chooses to change, it will be because of his or her own free will, and not because of coercion on your part. Each partner is totally responsible for his or her own changes. You cannot make the changes for someone else. Each person must choose his own.

In a limited partnership, a man and woman enter the marriage as *equals*. The strength in such a relationship is that you stay in it because *that is your desire*, because you feel that enough of your high priority needs are being met to make the relationship worthwhile.

Limited Partnership Advantages

The limited partnership presents numerous advantages over the fulfilled, or traditional, marriage. The limited partnership is:

- Realistic;
- Flexible;
- Exciting;
- Conducive to change and growth for both partners;
- Renewable and adaptable, it can accommodate the needs of both partners;
- Committed to the idea that both partners are equal.

A limited partnership allows for great freedom. Compare this with the fulfilled marriage, which provides very little freedom outside the marriage relationship.

We described the fulfilled marriage as a circle within a circle, with almost complete overlap. In the limited partnership, the amount of overlap between you and me is flexible and changeable. It allows for separateness, for individuality to express itself. A sizable portion of each circle always remains independent, self-sufficient and outside the relationship, as shown here.

As you can see from the figure on the following page, the limited partnership allows each of you many freedoms to seek satisfaction of needs that cannot be fulfilled by your partner, areas of mutual independence from traditional husband/wife roles.

Perhaps, for example, you are a woman with important professional skills. The limited partnership should allow you full freedom to practice those skills without threatening the male partner (the traditional breadwinner). Both partners should be free to cultivate outside friendships..

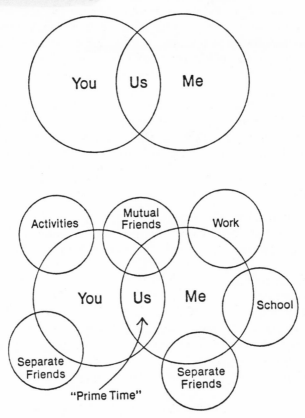

A husband may be a movie fan while his wife prefers opera and ballet. Rather than each insisting the other take part in his or her preferred activities, each may go to the movies or opera alone, or find other friends with whom to share the experience.

There is a multitude of such examples, in which each person may wish to go his or her way from time to time. But the heart of the relationship lies in the couple's commitment to give their best time and energy to each other.

In a limited partnership, the separate portions can reach out in as many directions as necessary at any given time. Activities, friends, school, and so forth are always secondary to the relationship. The "quality time" or prime time, as shared *within* the marriage relationship, is of primary importance.

It is not a question of who has more activities outside the marriage. It is not a competition of winners and losers or a game of one-upmanship. The extensions and the outside activities relate to the *needs* of each partner. Naturally, these needs vary from time to time. Limited partnership encourages the person to fulfill his needs. Some needs are fulfilled outside the marriage and some with the partner. Each person is nurtured in such a relationship.

The "Dead" Marriage

Sometimes the partners in a marriage are not relating in either a fulfilled style or a limited partnership style. They're not relating very much at all. This is often referred to as a dead marriage.

In this arrangement, the partners are superficially cordial, but distant. Their conversation focues around trivia and they experience no quality time together. Their daily encounters are reduced to rituals. Their dialogue narrows to statements such as, "How are you?" or "Did you have a good day?" or "What are we having for dinner?" There is little intimacy between them. Their sexual relations are infrequent and mechanical. There is much submerged resentment, passivity, and unexpressed anger in this non-relationship relationship. The two people have resigned themselves to performing expected duties and leading a generally unfulfilled life.

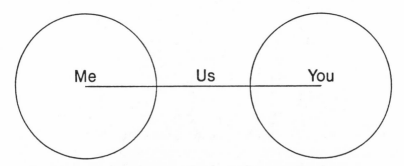

Why do people remain in such a relationship?

Some are frightened of being alone. The unskilled, nonprofessional woman will stay in the marriage because of material dependency. She may accept her lot passively, or someday may try to change the relationship by seeking professional counsel. The man will often state that he is all right, that the problem rests with his wife, and that there is nothing wrong with the marriage.

You may ask yourself, "How can he be so unaware?" The issue may not be lack of awareness. Perhaps he feels genuinely satisfied with the marriage. Often, also, the man receives the extra strokes and recognition he needs from his job. The nonworking homemaker ussually has no access to such emotional satisfaction.

What will happen to the dead marriage if both partners are not willing to revitalize it?

It will probably come to an end. The partners will not even experience a phase of mourning. The relationship may have been buried and the epitaph read many years ago.

Reasons for dissolving a dead marriage might be a new attachment outside the marriage for one of the partners, or completion of the parenting role when the last child leaves home. It often requires such a change or crisis for two people to recognize if their marriage has died or if it is possible to resurrect it.

Your Marriage Style Evaluation

Now that you have seen the different marriage styles — fulfilled marriage, limited partnership, and dead marriage — it is time to take an inventory of your own marriage style. Here are some guiding questions. Answer "Okay" or "Not Okay" to each one.

1. Do you have meaningful contact with each other on a daily basis? (This means communication about needs, wishes, and desires, not just chit-chat.)
2. Do you have at least a weekly meaningful contact with each other?
3. Are you able to express your satisfactions and dissatisfactions to each other?
4. What are your expectations of your duties in the house?
5. Have you discussed your attraction to people of the opposite sex openly?
6. Do you feel that in your marriage sexual relations are discussed and agreed upon?
7. How do you feel about your partner's needs to have separate activities during the day; for example, continuing education, sports activities, involvement with friends, going away alone, or going away on vacation or a professional convention?
8. How do you feel about your needs to have separate activities during the day?
9. How do you feel about each of you having separate activities at night; such as school, sports, friends, or other such activities?
10. How do you feel about your partner having a friend of the

opposite sex? How do you feel about them going out for lunch, going out in the evening, or going away for the weekend?

Perhaps it is unnecessary to say that you and your partner must be careful to be totally honest with yourself and with each other in answering these and other questions posed throughout the book. After you have answered these — and your partner has done the same, *separately* — compare your feelings about your marriage style. Make notes in your workbook about your partner's as you go along.

As to your marriage style, if you find that you are doing nearly everything together out of a sense of duty, and do not allow each other to pursue your own individual interests, then you have a *fullfilled* marriage in the sense described earlier in this chapter.

If, on the other hand, you spend prime time together while allowing your partner to pursue his or her own personal interests, then you have what we defined as a *limited partnership*.

And, if you find that you're not relating at all, you have a *dead* marriage. (Incidentally, if you and your partner were able to communicate with each other effectively in discussing the contents of this chapter, it's an initial indication that your marriage contains a spark of life after all.)

It should be made clear, also, that any marriage style is fine so long as both partners are satisfied and happy. We are not trying to dictate a way of life to you. You should lead the kind of life that is comfortable for *you*.

Now you've determined the type of marriage style you are leading. Are you happy with it? Do you want to make some changes? Are you both willing to work at it? Where do you go from here?

Do not try to make many major changes all at once.

If you try to change too much too quickly, you will not be successful. More likely, you will throw up your hands and quit trying. Obviously, this does not lead to your original goal of trying to improve your marriage, which can be done only if you move gradually and methodically.

The Myths and Realities of Marriage

Expectations are built on myth. That is why they are complex and difficult to change. Every person subscribes to many myths, the elusive wisps of dream and imagination that are part of our human makeup. While myths and expectations are wonderful creations of the human mind, they can also portray an idealistic objective which is realistically impossible to achieve. And when the person does not achieve his or her expectation, or when reality pales compared to the myth, the consequences are usually destructive.

Mythical Expectations

An important distinction must be drawn between expectations based on role concepts, and those based on myths. Much popular literature on the changing styles of marriage now focuses on roles: who will earn the money, who will make the beds, who will diaper the baby, who will mow the lawn. Discussion and definition of roles before marriage is healthy and beneficial, but the hidden "time bomb" remains if myths aren't explored and brought into focus. Even the man and woman who enter a marriage with total agreement about the roles of husband and wife can still harbor unreal expectations. These are most often rooted in the following myths:

Myth #1: Love will conquer all.

Love will continue without any attempts to nourish it. Love is magically present or tragically absent. Attempts to "construct" love are cold, mechanistic, lacking in spontaneity, and, therefore, somehow inappropriate.

Here is an example of this myth, which holds that it is enough to be in love and that everything else will authomatically fall into place in the relationship if you only possess that one key.

Judy has been married for more than a year. She is unhappy. During most of the time they have been married, her husband hss not talked about his feelings for her. He comes home tired, checks the mail, reads the paper, and gets ready for dinner. She is waiting for a sign of personal praise or recognition, but receives none. She tries to draw him out with positive comments but he does not respond. So Judy has decided it's no use and has withdrawn into herself, disillusioned and disappointed.

In this case, Judy made the mistake of assuming that the ardor of premarital love would continue into the marriage, lifting them as a couple above the commonplace problems of the world. Her husband, David, made the false assumption that his wife would know, without being told, that his love was strong and enduring. As he went about his work, which he considered an expression of his love, he did not understand that the strength of love comes from continued constructive actions by both parties.

Love does not conquer all other needs. Judy needs to know that David loves her, to be *told* now and then that what she is doing pleases or displeases him. She also needs reaffirmation that other aspects of their lives are fulfilled, and that David comes home because he is happy to be with her and to talk to her.

Love — like any other living thing — must be nourished. A vital relationship requires constant attention, dedication, and work. Effort devoted to a relationship brings many rewards, if it is *mutual* effort. Perhaps because of their social conditioning, women are more likely than men to acknowledge that they must "make an effort" to keep the relationship alive. However, this effort is often directed toward personal appearance alone. Or toward being a "good wife" — that is, living up to a stereotype. Neither of these efforts really comes to grips with the need to nourish the *interaction* between husband and wife as unique individuals.

The husband must also contribute. Many husbands may realize the necessity for this, but lack the skills to do it. Traditionally, men neglect this area because social stereotypes have implied that it is primarily the woman's obligation to adapt to her husband's needs. Preoccupation with romantic interaction has typically been a feminine trait. While love cannot be created simply by an act of will, some ingredients of love — respect, friendship, companionship, nurturing, communication, helping, and excitement — can be cultivated. And love does not exist as an entity unto itself. Partners must each make a daily *decision* to love, if love is to continue.

Myth #2: Sexual attraction will continue at a high level of intensity.
Sex will be fantastic all the time. If sex isn't excellent at first, it will become so through practice. In a good marriage, sex is super all the time.

The great amount of attention devoted to sexual matters in recent years has resulted in deep concern over the frequency of sexual intercourse. Many couples fear their marriage is "sliding downhill" if sexual relations occur less frequently as the years pass. This can result in a sense of obligation to keep up the pace in order to maintain a good marriage, and sex becomes a chore, making matters worse.

One couple I've counseled has been married for fifteen years.

Helen, who always has been motivated to "satisfy" her husband, was concerned that she and John were not making love as frequently as in the early years of marriage. More and more often, John was tired or failed to maintain an erection during intercourse. Helen worried that he no longer loved her.

After I encouraged them to examine and discuss the situation together, both came to realize that they had fallen into routine patterns of lovemaking and that John's capacity for sexual intercourse would naturally decline with age. I also encouraged this couple to experiment with different techniques of lovemaking, and to stress *quality* of *loving*, rather than *frequency* of love*making*. They found new depths of enjoyment in each other, especially when John was reassured that it was not always necessary for him to "produce on demand."

Sexual anxiety also results from current myths about how a woman must respond or what a man must produce. The game becomes one of counting climaxes or measuring erections. A woman who does not reach climax may fake it, an act which diminishes her own honest enjoyment of sexual tenderness. Or, she may blame her husband for not "giving her" a climax. Or the man may blame her. Because achieving climaxes has become the be-all and end-all of sexual contact, anxiety results. This anxiety leads to finding fault with a partner. Once one starts blaming the other for the absence of a woman's climax or the insufficiency of the man's erection, the marriage is headed for trouble.

Myth #3: You can keep the "spark" in your marriage forever.

Only those who don't love each other any more lose the spark. If the spark is gone, your marriage is dead.

When people talk of keeping or losing the spark, they are referring to the original attraction which drew them together. The spark is one of those vague ingredients of mythical expectation. Marriage is seldom as exciting as the first date. It cannot always retain the igniting spark because infatuation, the specific compulsion and excitement of a new relationship, is based on the thrill of discovery, of meeting a stranger and coming to know a person.

Many people want to know how to bring back the spark into their marriage. They are disappointed when they learn, realistically, that this can't be done. Once you know a person intimately, you can't retain the thrill of newness and discovery. It is a contradiction in terms. Once you have lived together for five, ten, or twenty years, you cannot retrieve the experience of first living together. Moments, and years, pass. If you must have the continuous excitement of new

21

love, the only way to find it is to move from one relationship into another. You cannot have both a life of "new love" and a lasting, intimate relationship; you must choose one or the other.

However, you need not give up the possibilities of a rewarding marriage when you relinquish your craving for the original spark. You can find or create new excitement. You can savor each portion, each new phase, of your life together.

In parenthood, for example, you start something new, unknown, and creative. When you move to a new house or city, you have a new life to carve out together. When your children leave home, you have an opportunity to experiment with lifestyles, travel, new freedom together. If you seize each moment in a long, well-known relationship, and bring to it the joint creation of something new, you will find that you have no cause to mourn the inevitable passing of the spark that lit the fire in the first place.

Myth #4: A good marriage is totally harmonious.

You are never justified in disagreeing with your partner. Your partner is never justified in disagreeing with you.

Human relationships as intimate and intense as marriage can never be totally harmonious. Yet, many marriages pictured by Hollywood, on television, or in children's books, are sweet, loving, and free of conflict. Naturally, children pick up the idea from these sources that the "normal" marriage is uniformly harmonious. Some children may temper this picture with their own family experience, or they may have trouble reconciling the two views.

If a family is reasonably happy, the child has a model against which to compare fiction. However, most children do not come from happy homes. The divorce rate is one proof of this; and if we are to assume that many parents stay together only "for the sake of the children," we can conclude that many newlyweds today were children in an unhappy family only yesterday. Unhappy homes make children insecure and unhappy. The child in such a home is likely to vow to himself that his own marriage will be different. The child vows that *his* marriage will be happy; *he* will avoid the mistakes of his parents; *he* will love without ever hurting; *he* will make his partner happy, and his partner will make him happy.

In making these vows, the child commits himself to the impossible. Since he has no model of a real-life, happy family, he constructs the fantasy of a happy family in his mind. Later, when he or she marries, the wonderful intentions are all geared to achieve the impossible. A person becomes hurt, angry, and disappointed when the reality of marriage does not measure up to the myth-fed fantasy.

A person then may feel "obligated" to get a divorce, reasoning that to remain in a disappointing marriage would be to admit that he could not do better than his parents.

It is far better to understand that happiness does not imply or require perfection. Nor is it necessary to squelch negative feelings. One cannot always avoid hurting a partner. Feelings that are bottled up — whether negative *or* positive — create tension that is potentially explosive in a marriage.

Myth #5: Fighting is irrational.

There are solutions to all problems if you are only calm and rational about things. A person who is irrational is wrong. Don't ever disagree.

This commitment to rationality runs afoul of reality very quickly. Sometimes there are no rational reasons for the motivations, preferences, desires, and feelings that come into conflict. Human beings don't always have reasons for the way they behave. What may seem trivial to you may be important to your spouse. Your values may simply be different. Your spouse might lose his patience and explode about things that in your mind are insignificant or stupid. There's the classic example of the mate who insists on squeezing the toothpaste from the middle of the tube. One might become annoyed because the other leaves shoes by the side of the bed. (The mate doesn't see anything wrong with this since the shoes will be put on again the next morning!)

Some couples never get over this stage of the relationship. The world is full of couples who, after twenty years of marriage, are spitefully arguing and, when they are not arguing, are carrying a load of feelings of irritation, hostility, and resentment.

Couples cannot expect rational solutions to all of their conflicts. The differences between two people are usually based upon different emotional responses to a situation. You can't ignore those differences simply because they are irrational, and you cannot eliminate them by trying to reason with each other.

Everyone is irrational about some preferences and dislikes in life. Often habits are acquired from childhood behavior that was approved by parents. An adult, so conditioned, then derives a sense of comfort from doing things in a certain way, and his or her way of doing things may well be irrational. Thus, no one in a marriage is "right" or "wrong," and conflict is not resolved by proving one is right and the other wrong.

Being calm and reasonable in decision-making is often important. But learning to fight is also important, and is necessary to resolve many conflicts. Solutions to some problems will come only through fighting.

Fights, of course, should be strictly limited to the immediate issues at hand, and not used as a dumping ground — by either partner — for all the other irritations that may have accumulated over the years of a marriage. Fight about one thing at a time, and force yourselves to *agree* on the limits before you start. Surprisingly, such an agreement often eliminates the need to fight in the first place.

Myth #6: *Your marriage should be "normal."*

Many couples confronting marital difficulties seek a solution by asking: "What is normal?"

Unfortunately, there is no objective measure of a "normal" marriage. In fact, if we look for an *average* marriage, the divorce rate is evidence that the average marriage is unhappy.

The best thing is to forget about external standards. Focus on your own priorities and values. The amount of conflict or communication that is right for your relationship is whatever makes you feel comfortable. YOU. Not a stereotyped image which you believe should be your yardstick.

Although we cannot discuss a normal marriage, we *can* set for ourselves the goal of a *healthy* marriage. A healthy relationship is one in which two people level with each other. In a healthy relationship, the partners' deal with each other as equals rather than attempt to manipulate each other, dominate, or play games. A healthy relationship is based upon openness and trust.

Myth #7: *Marriage will remove your feelings of worthlessness.*

You will find compensation for the lack of love in your earlier life.

This is a forlorn hope, because it can never be completely fulfilled. And, if you subsequently blame your partner — or your marriage — for your unfulfilled hopes, you are on the road to disaster.

Many people have suffered a painful lack of love from parents in childhood. Love deprivation causes insecurity and yearning for an all-encompassing, unconditional love which will fill the emptiness. This is a longing for *parental* love, and a marriage partner can never give you something missing from years ago, because those years have passed. No matter how much a person now loves you, he or she cannot erase years of longing. You will always feel like the child who was unloved by your parents. You cannot change the fact that they did not love you, or did not express their love clearly to you.

24

The task in marriage is to focus on what you have *now*. Focusing on adult love will at least help to dissolve a continuing sense of suffering. Don't ask your spouse to be the parent to a child who suffered long ago; ask him to love the person who exists now.

If you suffer from feelings of worthlessness or self-hate, your self-esteem is low. If your feeling of worthlessness is strong, do not expect your partner's love to automatically supply you with a feeling of self-worth. Love can ease the pain and help you to find the courage to work through your own problems. It does not deliver absolute self-esteem and happiness. You must save yourself.

Some young men and women marry at an early age to escape their parents and an unhappy family situation. Such marriages often fail. Here we find a person, or both persons, desperately hoping that marriage will be the solution to unhappiness. There is no assurance that it will be. Such a marriage is especially problem-filled when the unhappy person has low self-esteem, and, therefore, chooses a partner who is really unsuitable. This commonly happens because an individual's low self-esteem causes him to feel, "I don't deserve better." Thus, a sensitive and intelligent man might marry a coarse and dull woman, or vice versa. They are mismatched from the beginning, and so their relationship can never be one of full sharing and growth. In fact, if this man comes to a point later in life where his self-esteem improves, he finds himself in a situation where he must either reconcile himself to divorce, or live out life with an unsatisfying marriage.

In all marriages, we seek to move from myth to reality.

The Realities of Being Married

Marriage is *not* a myth. Marriage is not an answer to unfulfilled expectations. Marriage probably is not what you thought it would be.

What, then, is marriage, and what are the realities of being married?

Marriage is an expression of intimacy, security, companionship, and love. Marriage can, and should, be beautiful. It begins with two people falling in love and experiencing the wonderful feelings that they can share a life of love with each other. Unfortunately, problems often arise when romantic feelings collide with the daily realities of living together.

25

Obligations and Security

Sharing a life of love is what marriage can be. But one of the realities of marriage is that many people stay in a relationship when it is no longer satisfying. Why is this so?

Some people stay married out of a sense of obligation to their religion, to their children, or to their partner. Others remain in an unhappy situation because they have low self-esteem, which convinces them that they really don't deserve a better marriage than they have. Low self-esteem also fosters a feeling of hopelessness, a sense of despair over the possibility of improving life. This can manifest itself in overt cynicism, wherein the individual bitterly concludes that the reality of marriage is frustration, and it is, therefore, futile to exchange one relationship for another. This lack of self-esteem by one or both partners is a major cause of marital problems. It is important that each partner feel a healthy level of self-assurance before and during a relationship.

Individual needs are numerous and complex. One reason that two people enter a relationship is a desire for security. Conversely, many people stay in unsatisfying relationships because of insecurity, whether it be material, emotional, or intellectual. Let's examine each of these briefly.

Material Insecurity

At least until recent years, women were conditioned from childhood to see their role in life as wives and mothers. Few went to college to prepare for careers. As a result, they were afraid to consider being single and afraid of material insecurity. Obviously, then, when they entered a marriage, such women could not function as equal partners. Conflicts were generally resolved by feminine submission to the male point of view. Because of their material dependency, such women lost a measure of what was fair – their equal rights in a marital relationship. Eventually they even lost the capacity to realize the imbalance between the positive and negative aspects of their marriage. They came to accept everything as "normal."

Even today, when divorce is commonplace, insecurity is a common motive for a person to remain in an unhappy marriage, especially if there are children. Some women still feel insecure about their ability to support themselves, particularly if their education was interrupted by pregnancy and child-rearing. If such a woman pursues career training, once her children have left home or entered school, her insecurity over survival needs may be reduced. It is not surprising that many women terminate their unhappy marriages at this point.

Emotional Insecurity

Traditionally, women have also been more emotionally insecure than men. This is because until recently women were taught that their role in marriage was to be submissive and inferior to their husbands. Women were afraid to act or feel equal because it just was not part of the stereotyped role concept of the "positive wife." In a way, marriage gave women material security, while increasing their emotional insecurity!

The advent of the women's liberation movement is creating a positive change in the way many women perceive themselves. However, even the relatively liberated woman – and man – seems to be influenced in her or his choice of partner by the traditional tendency of women to marry men who are older, better educated, and perceived as being more intelligent than themselves. Many men still choose wives who are younger, shorter, less educated, and perceived as being less intelligent than themselves. (This tendency is generally used to explain why many intelligent and successful women are single – their male peers have chosen women "beneath" them.) The persistence of this mating gradient could perpetuate a tendency for women to feel inferior to their husbands – after all, they chose their man because they perceived him to be superior.

It is apparent, therefore, that as more women achieve better education and more equality in all areas of life, this aspect of emotional insecurity will be ameliorated. It has been my clinical observation that a woman who comes into a marriage with her own profession suffers less from both emotional and material insecurity. It seems that the knowledge that she *could* provide for herself if need be, and that she *chooses* her role freely in the relationship, enhances her sense of personal worth and independence.

Intellectual Insecurity

It is interesting that many women know that they are as intelligent or knowledgeable as their husbands, but regard this as their personal *secret!* The stereotype of a "good" wife has been that she does not disagree with her husband, certainly not in public. However, she should be challenging enough in her conversation to be *interesting to him*. The power of this expectation can be seen in husbands who are shocked, angered, or irritated if their wives disagree with their opinions on "intellectual" matters such as politics or economics. The man frequently assumes that his wife has made a total commitment to his intellect and his judgment.

27

Women, because of their social upbringing, frequently need to see the husband as the strong one — the rock of Gibralter, *their* strength. Even when a man is in fact a weak individual — insecure, neurotic, and unsure of himself — his wife may treat him like a king. Some women need to pretend to themselves that they have a strong husband, denying his weaknesses. Others attempt to help their man to be strong, because they see his weakness and are terrified. In either case, the relationship is brittle, and locked into a pattern of dishonesty.

So a fundamental reality of marriage is that it should not be based upon security needs, but rather upon equality, creativity, and intimacy.

Creative Marriage: Intimacy

In a creative marriage, an intimate relationship develops between two people who continue to grow, individually and as a pair.

You cannot relate to your partner intimately, or enjoy and appreciate his or her full intimate expression, if you don't like yourself. Liking yourself is where intimacy between two begins. It begins with the intimacy of one. By this I do not mean narcissism, but rather a realistic appreciation of your own self-worth.

Equality and *mutual commitment* are the keys to real intimacy with another person. *Connectedness* (the emotional feeling of specialness that exists between partners) plus *stability* and *permanence* are present in direct proportion to the feelings of mutual closeness and personal growth. You are *vulnerable* when you expose your weaknesses and your needs to another person. You are *exclusive* when you are not willing to share your intimate needs with your partner or anyone else.

Each person needs to know that he or she is the most important, the most special friend of the partner. Both have established their highest priority as being *with* and *for* each other. Also their availability to each other is higher, and takes precedence over availability to anyone else. Intimacy is a *choice*, and intimacy between partners is subject to vulnerability to, and rejection by, the other.

Partnership through Choice

The concept of choice is essential to the realities of marriage. The commitment starts with the choice two people make to be together, the choice of a partner who is to become the most significant associate in life.

Commitment is a free choice that *each person continues to make throughout the marriage*. At the same time, husband and wife both enjoy the freedom of individual feelings and the expression of those feelings, whether positive or negative. That is, the freedom to be *you*.

If you recognize that the commitment to marriage is *always* a commitment by choice, you are also ready to see marriage as a union of *equals*. Equality is one of the essential realities in a successful, creative marriage. Equals take risks in being honest with each other, in expressing the need to feel secure. Expressing such needs also makes you vulnerable if you are dependent for emotional or material survival upon your partner. Yet it is the willingness to take this risk that leads to genuine intimacy.

Equals have the strength to assert themselves, to express disagreements, to fully experience their humanness — and to ask for help. For a marriage in which two equals feel free to continue growing separately as well as together, *trust* in one's self and one's partner is essential.

Now, let's look at some of the other realities of marriage. (For further discussion of the realities of marriage, refer to *Changing Your Lifestyle* by Frieda Porat, Ph.D., and Karen Myers.)

Reality #1: We are not in love all the time.

We move into and out of a relationship in a certain rhythm, and the rhythm is ours. At times we feel very close, loving, and intimate, but a short time later we can feel contented although separate and distant from our partner. This does not mean that we stop caring and loving; it only means that the relationship changes in intensity as the moods of the partners change. This is a normal and natural fluctuation.

Give yourself permission *not* to feel that you must be close all the time, not to feel obligated, and not to feel that it is a duty to love. These self-imposed demands can destroy the freedom to be yourself. You — with mood swings, ups and downs — and your partner with his or her individual pace, will flow toward and away from one another within a healthy relationship.

Reality #2: We cannot fulfill all the needs of our partner.

In an intimate relationship, each of us is limited in our ability to fulfill what our partner needs in life. You are not the mirror image of the person you marry. Two people never have exactly the same interests or capacities. Respect your partner for what he is, see him

29

for *who* he is rather than trying to change him. We are all different. Accepting and respecting the differences between yourself and your partner is the only way a marriage can continue.

Consider the wide range of human needs — intellectual, professional, emotional, spiritual, and physical. To expect one person to provide stimulation and satisfaction in all these areas is unrealistic and futile. One partner, for example, might need intellectual discussion in areas where the spouse is ignorant or uninterested. It is important to look for the fulfillment of such a need within oneself or in other resources, such as friends, lectures, books, or classes, rather than to view the partner as inadequate or inferior.

A person may have emotional needs which the partner either cannot, or chooses not to, fulfill. A wife, as an example, may need a listener, someone to listen to an expression of feelings pent up over a long period of time. If the partner is not happy or comfortable in the role of listener, he is justified in declining to hear her out. There are other ways to deal with and to express feelings. Share them with a friend, for example, or express them in a group encounter. Write them down in a journal, or express them in other art forms.

Many couples do not share the same interest in sports or other physical activities, such as dancing, hiking, or swimming. You can each fulfill your own needs alone or join a club or class to find people with whom to share these activities. Again, don't expect your partner to share naturally all of the physical activities that interest you.

A special physical need is sexual expression, which evokes exceptional rules and commitments in marriage. Unless *both* partners choose a marriage style wherein sex is not exclusive with the marriage partner, sex will be an expression of total intimacy which cannot include others. For this reason, sexual activity and communication require special nurturing. Both partners must be committed to their sexual evolution as a couple. Sexual interrelation is both intense and troublesome for many couples.

Reality #3: Most disagreements and differences between partners can be resolved through compromise.

Most disagreements do not stem from one person being right and the other wrong. The goal, then, is to find a solution that two people can accept and which allows them to live comfortably without sacrificing or changing themselves to the point where they resent the relationship. Many issues are trivial. And many marriages break up because of the inability to compromise on trivia.

Here are some of the trivial complaints I have heard shouted by two people, just before divorce:

> "Why don't you keep your clothes more tidy?"
> "Why are you always late?"
> "Why is dinner never ready on time?"
> "Why am I always the one to give in?" (Or "to plan the week-
>   end?" or "to take out the garbage?")

The list of such minor, but irritating, complaints is endless, and here is where you can begin using your notebook. Write down a list of small things your partner does regularly that irritate you. Then exchange lists with him or her. You may be surprised — and even amused — when you express your feelings by writing the list and then by reading the things that irritate your spouse. Bringing such things out into the open can help to relieve the sting.

The art of marriage depends upon the ability to say, "You do it this way, I do it my way. Let's find a solution in which both of us can continue living together without being annoyed with each other about these issues." Here is the essence of a workable compromise and you will have the opportunity, by working with this book, to practice the art of compromise.

As you see, disagreeing about trivial matters is common in marriage. Paradoxically, most couples cope much better with the big issues in their lives, such as moving to a new house, caring for a sick child, or changing jobs. Repeated small irritations are the ones that most generally cause you to lose patience.

Reality #4: We are not perfect.

No one is perfect. We are neither entirely strong nor totally weak, all giving nor all taking. We are all of these things at different times to varying degrees. Learning to accept the range of qualities in a partner, and not to make judgments about that person, is to acknowledge the existence of a real person, and not a stereotype or model.

Each person has many positive qualities to offer, qualities that most likely accounted for the initial attraction between partners. Each of us can choose to focus on the positive elements we give to and receive from each other, the pleasures we get and give, and at the same time to accept the shortcomings of the other. After all, to see a fault in a partner involves a subjective judgment on your part. If your partner feels comfortable in the ways she does things, the ways in which she functions and relates to you, learn to accept the person as she is.

31

Can You Live with the Realities?

No one but you can decide if you will be able to live with the realities of being married. You must decide that for yourself. You must look at the advantages and disadvantages to *you* of being married. And you must look at the advantages and disadvantages of being single. You must look at the investment that is necessary to make a marriage work and decide whether or not the investment will pay off for you.

The Mini-Contract

So you are not perfect and neither is your partner. Before you start learning the skills for maintaining a good marriage, you need to make a joint decision and an agreement to work at it sincerely *for at least three months*. This is the first mini-contract between you and your partner. It must include the following elements:

1. You will put time aside — *prime* and *committed* time — to work alone and with your partner, twice a week, for one to two hours at a time.
2. You will work with your partner and spend fifteen minutes each day answering the questions at the end of the chapters in this book. After you answer the questions alone, you will then share your answers with your partner.
3. At this point, you *rethink* — that is, change your attitude, and practice the new attitude. Remember to praise your partner as he or she is trying to make changes in behavior. A word of praise can go a long way, especially in trying to encourage *new* behavior.
4. After you come to a workable conclusion, then move on to the next chapter of the book.

You may decide the speed of your own program, and some chapters of the book will require more attention than others, but I would recommend spending about a week per chapter. This will set out for you a ten- to twelve-week program which corresponds roughly to the term of your first mini-contract. If you both agree to learn and practice the skills covered in the chapters to come, I am confident that you will enrich your marriage without the help of a professional counselor in private sessions.

Remember to use your notebook at all times — not only for the questions and answers, but to jot down ideas, new insights, and feelings which come to you as you work together. Divide the notebook into sections according to book chapters, and then devise whatever work system feels comfortable.

Mini-Contract Sample

I, _____, promise I am willing to devote the necessary time and energy to explore my relationship with _____, my partner.

I am willing to:
> learn new skills,
> practice new skills,
> continue a maintenance program,
> spend two hours per week with my partner going over material in this book.

I am also willing to be:
> honest,
> open,
> nonattacking,
> nondefensive,
> a participant in conflict resolution.

I am willing to give up old:
> outdated scripts,
> false expectations,
> ineffective habits,
> stereotypic ways of thinking,
> destructive behavior.

I am ready to learn new:
> scripts,
> realistic expectations,
> attitudes,
> positive thoughts,
> constructive behavior.

Signed _____

_____

Date_____
Witnessed by _____(a friend)

Now you are ready to begin. With a positive attitude, you will achieve what you want.

Merging Myths and Realities

Remember, one of the most important things we are trying to do at this point is help you to step away from the myths from the past, and to create new realities for yourself and your partner. Although the process is simple, most people must invest considerable time and patience to make the required changes. Briefly, these are the steps you will go through.

1. *Recognize your own unrealistic expectations.* Do you expect your wife to be always charming, beautiful, and well-groomed despite the work she has been doing throughout the day? Do you expect your husband to be always strong, wise, understanding and protective? Do you expect your sex life to be always perfect? These are just a few of the possibilities.

2. *Identify what your partner is capable of changing and willing to change.* Does your wife clutter the bathroom with laundered nylons? Does your husband leave tools strewn around the garage floor and driveway? Start with the small ones and work up to the big ones.

3. *Identify the areas that you are not willing to change or are not capable of changing.* Does your husband drink so much that it worries you? Does your wife eat too heavily, gaining weight as she compensates for other frustrations? Do you both stubbornly insist that you deserve such small pleasures from life?

4. *Work out compromises that are agreeable to each partner.*

Do *not* try to work on all irritating facets at once. Take one compromise at a time and the next one will be easier. Remember, as we work through the book chapter by chapter, you will be receiving additional guidance in each step.

An Exercise to Break Down the Myths of Marriage

Now you can begin to examine your own myths about marriage. Complete the following exercises.

A. Write down in your notebook all the statements you can think of about what you believe to be the perfect marriage. Then, in the columns to the right, write down the source of each notion; that is, *who* told you this is what a marriage should be. You may want to use your own format, or the following examples may be helpful.

Remember, these are only examples. You and your partner should feel free to add as many items to the list as you wish and to express them in any way, using as many words as are necessary to make the thoughts clear. Above all, try to precisely identify the source of your notions of what a marriage should be.

	Source		
The Perfect Marriage	Parents	Self	Others
1. I should _____			
2. He (she) should _____			
3. The house we have should _____			
4. The jobs we have should _____			
5. The income we have should _____			
6. The friends we have should _____			
7. Sex should be _____			
8. The feelings between wife and husband should be ___ _____			
9. Marriage will bring _____ _____			
10. After I have been married for a while _____			

B. Compose another list that *describes your reality* — how your marriage really is, not how you think it should be. For every item you wrote in part A, write a similar item describing how things really are.

C. Compose a third list that focuses on the aspects of your marriage that *dissatisfy* you now. What are the things you don't like in your partner? What don't you like in yourself? What would you like to change in your marriage?

Include trivia as well as the items you consider more important. As you undertake this exercise, consider that someone has given you permission to write down all the things that have been bothering you. Remember, you have already signed a mini-contract with your spouse to explore these areas with the understanding that you are not trying to hurt each other. To help you get started, here are some beginning phrases to start you expressing feelings, observations, and comments.

1. I don't like my partner's _____
2. I don't like my _____
3. If my partner would only _____
4. If I could change five things about my partner, _____
    _____
5. If I could change five things about myself, _____
    _____
6. The thing that bothers me most _____
7. I wish he (she) would _____
8. I wish I would _____
9. I hate it when he (she) _____
10. I hate it when I _____
11. It bothers me when _____

> D. After you have completed the above lists (and be prepared that this may require several work sessions before you and your partner are finished with it), continue to write answers to the following questions in your workbook.

1. What were my expectations of marriage?
2. What did I expect from my partner?
3. What did I see as his (her) roles?
4. What personality did I hope he (she) should have?
5. How did I view love?
6. How did I feel about arguments, about fighting?
7. Did I feel our marriage would cure my hunger and need for self-esteem?
8. What choices have I made about our relationship in the marriage?
9. What are the commitments I made when we decided to get married?

As you can see, the previous lists and questions to answer represent work, but it is necessary work. The deeper you delve into your needs and feelings as you go along, the more beneficial this work will be.

After you finish writing, you'll probably heave a sigh of relief, but this is only the beginning.

Now trade lists with your partner. Once you have absorbed what he or she has written, discuss your lists point by point. As you discuss your own and your partner's myths and realities of marriage, the realities should emerge more clearly and you can begin to compromise and end the disparity between the two.

Perhaps you might even question whether your marriage style is right for you.

3 Dual-Career Marriage

In any relationship in which two people become one, the end result is two half people.

Wayne Dyer

The High-Tech advances in lasers, radar, satellites, and computers pervade our lives and change our perspectives in such subtle ways, we aren't conscious of the effects.

In the 1950's, the stereotyped role for women was housekeeper, mother, homemaker and submissive wife whose primary role was to compliment her husband. Few women worked. Working mothers were frowned upon. Today 70 percent of married couples both work. This change represents more than a 50 percent increase over the percentage of married women in the labor force in 1960.

This kind of explosive cultural change has occurred in a single generation. Although some women are happy as housewives, they often feel defensive. However, support groups to help women choose among many options make it possible for women to elect not to work for whatever periods of time they decide.

Both husbands and wives have begun to realize that marriages are more successful when both partners fulfill themselves and their potentialities. In the 1950's it took a courageous mother to say, "I work because I'm a happier person and a better mother than when I stay home."

Today it takes the same kind of courage for a wife to say, "I am happy and fulfilled as a housewife." With the freedom to choose, both men and women today can live the kinds of lives they want.

A recent nationwide survey of 680 married couples, conducted at the University of Illinois, shows that husbands and wives seem happiest if both have full-time jobs and they equally split up the routine chores of housework and child care.

Depression is most common when the wife has to work to make ends meet. She is particularly unhappy when both she and her husband wish she could stay home, and she still does all the housework. The study shows the husband in these marriages is even more likely to be depressed than his wife.

Work and Health

Ever since women began flooding the paid labor market twenty years ago, there has been speculation about how working would affect their health. There were three different theories.

One view suggested that women would eventually have the same health problems as working men: heart attacks, lung cancer, and stress-related diseases.

A second theory suggested women may be stronger biologically than men and would actually be healthier working outside the home. Their health would be enhanced by the stimulation, self-esteem, support and social contacts of the workplace.

A third supposition was that women would suffer from having to be all things to all people: working woman, homemaker, mother, wife. The pressure and demands for her to balance less time with more responsibility would increase stress and reduce leisure time — adversely affecting the health of the employed woman.

In the Michigan Panel Study of Income Dynamics, since 1968 5,000 people have been interviewed yearly on work-related problems. The researchers found that a woman with poor health to begin with is less likely to work and will work fewer hours. A woman with good health is more likely to work and to work more hours. The researchers found some surprising results:

- Work is not likely to lead to major deterioration in women's health.
- Work itself seems to be associated with an improvement in health.
- The hours spent in child care and housework are not generally a major factor in working women's health if the children are over six years of age..
- Working mothers with children under six years old have more health problems.
- Women who are self-employed are more likely to have

poorer health.
- Women who have been married for many years are less likely to have health problems.
- Women who smoke are likely to have health problems.

Although studies like this one may not fit an individual, it is encouraging in that it tends to show that work itself, if anything, leads to an improvement in health. Since our society is moving in the direction toward more women working, it's comforting to know that it won't have negative effects on the health of the majority of working women.

Work and Equality

During World War II, when many women worked while the men were overseas fighting, some women found they preferred work to staying home. However, most people in the 1940's disapproved of working wives. A woman's place was in the home. It took a lot of courage for a woman to defy the rules. It took a secure husband to allow his wife to work.

Alice Kelly is in her sixties. She laughs when people talk about dual-career couples. She says, "You'd think these young people had created something that never before existed. There are a few of us wives who have always worked. It was harder before it was the "in" thing to do. But I always worked and loved it."

Alice and Michael were twenty years old in December 1941 when the Japanese bombed Pearl Harbor. While Michael was overseas fighting the war, Alice finished college. When Michael came home, he transferred his skills as a mechanic on airplanes to working on autos. They had two children. When the children started school, Alice decided staying home all the time made her feel depressed and anxious.

Alice told Michael she wanted to be a teacher. Michael, an unusual man for his time, felt proud of his wife. Alice started teaching under an emergency credential while taking courses toward a master's degree in education.

In the morning, Michael would dress their six-year-old son while Alice dressed the four-year-old. While Alice made breakfast, Michael made sandwiches for lunches. While Alice washed the dishes, Michael wiped off the stove and refrigerator. They made the beds together. Before they both left for work at 7:30 A.M., the beds were made, the dishes were done, and the four of them walked out the door together.

Today, Alice says, "It was a routine full of satisfaction. We

41

never discussed who would do what. We just did it."

Michael and Alice were anachonisms for their time. Yet their kind of teamwork can be satisfying when a married couple treats each other as equals; when they both have mutual goals and values. Without knowing they were models of equality, Alice and Michael took pride in the unique qualities of their partner.

Reasons For Dual-Careers

Both men and women today realize and value their potential. They are reevaluating their own interests and needs. They give many reasons for wanting to be a working-married couple.

Sometimes one person in a marriage will work while the other completes an education. Sometimes they both work and take evening classes, simultaneously supporting each other if both want degrees. In the competitive work-world, advanced training and refresher courses are often required.

However, one common reason given for wanting to work is economic; such as, buying a home, saving for a new car, and generally upgrading the family's standard of living.

Caught in the national economic stagnation of the '70's at the same time they — and millions of their fellow baby boomers — entered the job market, many young professionals are actually worse off economically than their parents, according to a new study by economists for the Urban Institute of Washington, D.C.

Unlike their fathers, who could expect their earnings to increase by more than 60 percent between the ages of 30 and 40, men who turned 30 in 1973 saw their real income go up by an average of less than 1 percent over the next decade. Therefore, when couples say they work to upgrade their standard of living, their reasoning is based on fact.

Working couples must be flexible and willing to cope with constant change, to reorder their priorities whenever one or the other experiences time pressures, stress, and anxieties. These changes can best be incorporated into a marriage when both partners are aware of the pressures at the time they happen and are willing to discuss their feelings and thoughts.

Sometimes a husband feels uncomfortable watching his wife change. As he sees her become more competitive and collaborative with men, he longs for the dependent person she used to be when he was the center of her world. However, as he watches her excitement and growth, as her fulfillment enriches the marriage, he begins to adjust — even enjoy her metamorphosis.

42

At times when both partners voice their opinions, their unique needs, they are likely to face disagreement. Both will need to develop their communication and assertiveness skills. When one or the other "gives in" just to keep the peace, resentment can bury itself like the fires in a volcano.

However, on many issues only one person has strong opinions. For example, a wife doesn't like to decide where to go, what to do, or how to spend their social time. Fortunately, she chose a social mate who likes making those decisions. Or on another issue, the husband hates to balance the checkbook and take care of the finances. Since the wife considers herself especially skilled with money, she is willing to take care of the budget-balancing aspects of their marriage.

If each person values the partner as an equal and respects and cares for the personal growth of their partner, each will strive for some mutual compromises in their relationship that can accommodate them both.

Husbands and Housework

The one issue that many married, working couples find most difficult is balancing housework and family care. As women have entered the work force, they find themselves with two jobs — work and family. Basically husbands, according to research studies, are not sharing that load. Many of the men who do spend time caring for their children and pitching in on household tasks seem to be doing so not out of love and support for their wives but out of dissatisfaction with their spouses.

A three-year study of 160 middle-class families in a Boston suburb found the following:

- Fathers' participation in housework and child care is not affected by their wives employment. Men whose wives have outside jobs do not do more around the house than men married to full-time housewives.
- Mothers spend nearly twenty hours a week alone with their children; fathers spend little more than five hours a week.
- Only eleven out of 160 men took any responsibility for such "feminine" jobs as laundry and shopping for groceries.

In this study, the researchers found the greater a man's participation in family life, the more competent and involved he feels as a father, and the less sex-stereotyped are his children — especially his sons. The greater a man's participation in family life, the more likely he is to be satisfied with his marriage and with his wife's competence as a mother.

The familiar businessman's lament is, "I'd be more involved with my family, but I just don't have the time."

Fernando Bartolome, who is conducting research on the professional and private lives of executives says, "Explaining family difficulties in terms of work pressures doesn't hold water." He says, "The time most executives have available for their private lives is roughly equal to, if not greater than, the time they devote to work." He adds, "Workaholics, the exception, are prisoners of success." They are not trying to escape through work but are in love with the rewards of their jobs. As a result, they often neglect their private lives.

Although some men simply do not want to spend time taking care of children and doing housework, probably more of them feel incompetent as husbands and fathers. Since men generally have trouble talking about their feelings and fear conflict at home, they tend to let problems slide.

These same men who may be expert at solving work problems can learn to transfer those skills to solving family problems. Competence at marriage can be learned. The first step is to shed the fear that talking about important issues is too disruptive or threatening to the relationship. The second step is to stop putting off until it's too late what needs to be done today.

In many ways this social transition from housewife to working wife has been more difficult for men. Many men really want a wife like their mother who took care of them and their house. Their fathers didn't share housework and childcare. This whole cultural change feels like the rug under their feet has been yanked out.

Some men have gone so far as to search for Oriental wives through mail-order marriage brokers because they want submissive women who will make them the center of the family. However, once these young Oriental women are acculturated into the American society, they, too, become less submissive, often resulting in unhappy marriages.

Our culture today gives us all the choices we could want in lifestyle. Many single people have found that being single is a preference and does not mean they are incapable of loving or being loved. Being single is another option for those who do *not* value monogamy, compromise, partnership, and permanence.

Travel and Transfer Options

In business, some people prefer to be sole owners. Others find they can accomplish their goals faster and better in a partnership. Marriage is a partnership with both privileges and liabilities. The degree of equality varies in each marriage. One goal in a marriage partnership is to have two people who accept and share both the responsibilities and gains equally.

Janet and David are an example of equality in a partnership marriage. When Janet married David, he was a chemistry professor. Janet was educated at a finishing school and then graduated from Smith College with a degree in English literature. When she married David, Janet knew how to promote him as a respected member of the faculty community.

Charming and adept, Janet joined the hospital auxiliary and the Junior League. She became an active community member. Later, after their two children reached school age, Janet became restless. She said, "I felt like crawling the walls."

David encouraged Janet to go back to school. She enrolled as a full-time student at Stanford and earned a master's in business administration. It was a demanding program. David felt proud of his wife. She was an excellent student and graduated with honors.

Janet was offered three excellent positions. The one she liked best was in Washington, D.C. At this point, beginning her career, Janet was unwilling to suggest her husband leave his tenured position at the university and move to another city.

Both David and Janet realize that by increasing Janet's options, they have opened "a can of worms" that could, in the future, create real problems in the marriage.

Many families do, in fact, move from one place to another. The average American moves every five years. Children are automatically uprooted. Although some stress can accompany a move, children are as flexible as their parents. When a mother says, "Oh, my poor darlings, have to leave all their friends. . .", the children automatically pick up their mother's anxieties. If she says, "Moving is exciting. You will go to new schools and make new friends and see the world," children are more apt to respond positively to the change.

In contrast, Michael's mother and father wanted to give their child stability. They stayed in one house from the time he started school until he got to the sixth grade. They live near the Stanford Campus where graduate students with their children come and go from points all over the world. One day Michael said, "How come we never move. Everybody else does."

The point is we live in a fast-changing world with multiple

values and complex lifestyles. Our attitudes toward what is happening create our reality.

William James said, "The greatest discovery of our generation is that human beings, by changing the inner attitudes of their minds, can change the outer aspects of their lives."

Some dual-career partners have tried running two households in different cities and spending weekends together. For example, Pauline spends her working week in Seattle while her husband, Alan, works and lives in Portland. One weekend he drives to Seattle. The next weekend she drives to Portland. This kind of arrangement is temporary. They do not expect to live out their married lives in different cities. It works as long as they both agree to make it work.

Emotional Support

In secure marriages, exceptional couples who find their professions lucrative or fascinating enough, fly clear across the United States to spend vacations together. Both men and women in politics, at times, put their families on the back burner when state and national legislative bodies are in session.

Many executive women as well as women in politics have husbands who take pride in their wives contributions to the world. However, in the privacy of their own homes, these husbands and wives have painful conflicts and problems, as do every married couple.

At certain times in every marriage, the marriage agreements must be renegotiated. These times may come more rapidly in the dual-career partnerships because both partners will change more rapidly than if they stay with traditional roles.

If a couple finds satisfaction and stability in traditional roles, they will make sacrifices for their choices. If a couple decides to work toward equality, they must make different sacrifices which require constant renegotiation as they continue to change — both as a couple and as individuals.

The primary consideration is to know who you are and what you want, and to be aware when you have changed and when what you want has changed. Being aware of personal change is difficult. You get so used to being who you *were*, you often don't know when you have satisfied old needs and created new ones.

It is even more difficult to be in touch with changes in a relationship. In a partnership, people make joint decisions. If either a husband or wife receives an attractive, lucrative job offer with a large increase in salary, some partners will be willing to move. Others

46

will need time to work out a compromise. And some will simply find such changes as leaving non-negotiable. Each couple must find their own solutions to travel and transfer options when they occur.

Switching Roles

Two years ago, Tracy and Bill decided to trade places. Bill was laid off by Caterpillar Tractor just two weeks after Tracy's position as a part-time computer programmer turned into a full-time job. Now Bill stays home with Rachel, 7, and Nathan, 6 — while Tracy pursues her career. Bill says, "Boy, has this switch been an eye-opener!"

Bill has learned new respect for what a housewife does. He says he is not as good a housekeeper as his wife, but he cleans, cooks, and does the laundry. The role change has proved beneficial for the children. Bill used to leave for work in midafternoon and did not return until late in the evening. Now he meets the children after school, takes them for doctor and dentist appointments, and gets involved in their activities.

Bill says, "I feel closer to the children, and I think they're closer to me than before."

In a community where many men have been laid off, this couple is not alone in reversing roles. However, Bill does not like being unemployed. He hopes to be called back to work. Even then, Tracy will make more money than Bill. He says, "That's great! I just want a job, not a career."

Not all the problems of dual-careers must be solved. Many of them are temporary and change over time without any intervention.

Integrating Needs of Dual-Career Families

According to the Wall Street Journal, the "new drop-outs" are women who, after achieving a certain status in the corporate world, have found it impossible to combine career and child rearing. The Journal warned that this trend could undo some impressive gains women have made in the workplace.

The stresses of combining career and family are familiar both personally and professionally to many women. This problem is not simply a "couple's problem." Consulting groups work with both families and companies to develop new options for integrating the needs of dual-career families with those of the corporation.

The issue is a complicated one and is viewed differently by corporations and their employees. Companies are faced with requests for part-time work, flexible hours, and childcare.

Trying to hold down 60-hour a week jobs (not uncommon in a fast-track career) puts enjoyment of family on the back burner. There are no solutions that will solve everyone's problem. Although most people look at stresses as problems, another attitude is that they are opportunities.

A crisis is defined by the Chinese as "A Dangerous Opportunity." With the growing number of well-prepared young women who are launching corporate careers, companies sense they are sitting on a potential timebomb that will explode when job and family collide. Confronting these crises can lead to corporate and individual solutions.

Many corporate men have career wives. The company policy of transferring its employees to places with few opportunities for wives causes family problems. Companies must accommodate career couples or deal with a tremendous employee turnover rate.

Part-time and flex-time work is both expensive and aggravating for companies. However, turnover costs of replacing key employees is also high. Companies can lose money in lost potential when an experienced person leaves. The cost of the 60-hour work week, in terms of employee burnout, alcoholism, and so on, may be very high.

Many companies depend on a select talent pool. To limit that pool may be too costly. Several large companies have instigated childcare facilities near the job site. Although no one program will fit all companies, they are going to have to weigh flexibility losses against losing key personnel.

Balancing Time for Work, Family, and Self

Problem solving skills in the dual-career family is a joint venture between working couples and the companies they work for. Corporate day care centers will not fill the bill at all companies. Some companies will be better off with a voucher system for day care. Other will have a back-up system in which the company infirmary could accept a sick child who can't go to day care.

Some consultants are designing structures that will benefit companies and their employees. Individual plans might involve small changes such as adjusting hours — going back and forth between longer and shorter work weeks. After maternity or paternity leave, for example, a company might instigate a four-day work week as a temporary measure.

It is interesting to note that the Wall Street Journal article indicates that women who leave corporations because of career-family conflicts do *not* leave the workforce. Many start their own businesses which allows them to arrange more flexible hours.

Today our society accepts and encourages dual-careers. They can actually enhance a marriage. A working woman can bring excitement to the partnership. More importantly as a satisfied person, she and her husband can grow financially, intellectually, and emotionally while complementing one another.

Although there are no ideal dual-career arrangements, each couple must continuously communicate with each other. The following statements can serve as starting points. You and your spouse can separately write in your notebook responses to the following. Then you can share your responses.

- Tell your spouse that you are not asking him or her to change, that you are simply communicating what you appreciate and love and what you miss that you would like without any demands or expectations.
- From 1 (low) to 10 (high), tell your spouse how satisfied you are with the part you presently play in your marriage.
- Tell your spouse how you would like your life to be different.
- Tell your spouse three things you most enjoy and appreciate about him or her.
- Tell your spouse something you want that you are not getting from him or her.
- Tell your spouse what he or she might do that could make an unsatisfying situation better.

Sharing your thoughts and feelings does not mean that another person must meet your demands. Some things may not change. Some things will change. With some issues an acceptable compromise may be reached.

The various issues of dual-career couples are here to stay. We live in an era when the number of dual-career marriages is on the rise. Ultimately, there are no general rules for solutions. Each unique couple must work out its own personal solutions. Hopefully, each person will be committed to giving understanding and empathy to the other.

Underlying each crisis is an opportunity for growth and caring for the marriage partner. Ultimately, love is the overflow of our fulfillment that we give to others. Therefore, it is to the benefit of each person in any relationship to invest in the fulfillment of the other person.

4 Second Marriages and Blended Families

If marriages do not last forever,
then why should divorce?
Jean-Pierre Aumont

We live in a society that says "the good life" is falling in love, marriage for life with the love partner, good sex, and parenthood. Society tells us we can only love one man or one woman and that we should love that person forever. For many people, this fantasy creates more unhappiness than any other belief system with which we get indoctrinated.

In the final analysis, most wars begin with basic incompatibilities in personalities, values, and belief systems. In some cases, those basic differences cannot be resolved. The marriages must end for the emotional health and survival of the individuals.

The purposes for marriage are varied and complex. Marriages, for some individuals, provide sexual and social gratification, as well as the potential for financial and emotional security. Some individuals find, in marriage, incentives for growth and personal development. Those who have children transmit genes and culture. Marriages also provide for the needs of children as well as to establish hereditary lines.

In our culture, we believe in marrying for love. But we have different visions of what the word "love" means and how to demonstrate it. Few young people know that when you love someone, *you do not love them all the time* and that the love you feel changes over time.

Even when couples stay together for life, there is not just one marriage between a husband and wife, but many. They pass through many stages of the marital life-cycle. They are successively newlyweds, young parents of young children, older parents of adolescents, mutual victims of their mid-life crises, "empty nesters" when the children leave, and finally, senior citizens.

Each stage in the cycle overlaps with the preceding one and the one to come. We fail to notice the gradual changes as we pass from one stage to the next. However, each stage brings its unique conflicts and challenges, and each must be dealt with differently.

As the "honeymoon stage" fades, the passion between two lovers changes. Passion has a different value for different human beings. Some individuals yearn forever for the fantasy time of the fairytale Prince and his Cinderella.

Although some part of us longs for that first stage of love, in reality many anxious moments occur during that insecure honeymoon stage: the embarrassment of taking off clothes, of using the bathroom, of being unattractive in the morning.

However, we eventually let the passion go for marital love that develops when it joins hands with other emotions such as caring, affection, trust, and empathy. Even sex, we learn, can be a communion, an act of compassion and friendship.

Marriages are characterized by varying degrees of loyalty and disloyalty, cooperation and competition. In every loving relationship, we experience moments of being miserable, angry, lonely, afraid, and hostile. Yet, if negative emotions take over and fill every day, married life becomes intolerable. For some, the battle becomes a war. In other cases, the marriage dies a slow death.

Divorce

Those individuals who expect their marriage to be "perfect," to provide all of their needs – all the time, set themselves up for disillusionment, disappointment, and guilt.

When the weight of disappointment becomes too great – when guilt gets too heavy, we tend to blame someone or something outside ourselves. Because we don't want to believe we are *unloving*, we tend to project the fault onto others. We search for reasons, personality traits, weaknesses in a mate to which we attach blame. Secretly we fear we are *unlovable*.

"No Fault" divorce, as a legal form, recognizes that by virtue of being who they are, two people can be incompatible. Although some individuals choose, for a variety of reasons, to stay in a dead marriage, others refuse to die with the marriage.

When individuals get miserable enough, some decide to end the marriage. They mourn, go through denial and isolation, move in and out of anger and depression, and finally grow to accept the death of their marriage.

Others who fear change, even though their marriage doesn't work very well, cling to their unhappy lives. In one study of thirty-five couples married 50 years, 40 percent said they were happily married; 60 percent said they stayed together because they did not believe in divorce.

We have been programmed with the idea that "divorce is bad." Even a bad marriage, some people believe, is better than no marriage. Some churches have exerted destructive forces on divorce. Therefore, for a variety of reasons, many individuals live with an unhappy marriage rather than risk change. They preserve a facade and live with the status quo.

Our society tells you that divorce is equivalent to personal "failure." Therefore, since you are a product of your culture, you believe you have failed. Failure is a bitter pill. In defense, you mourn for the lost dreams, you cry in pain, you alternately hate yourself and then your spouse.

Before a divorce, most individuals go through long periods of unhappiness rather than admit failure. Others live with apathy. In most divorces, one person does the leaving and one person gets left. Regardless of who does what, divorce is one of life's most painful experiences.

In a divorce, there is no defined set of rules to help you solve your pain. The ways in which you cope with those pains will differ from how others cope. Prescribed solutions seldom work. But support groups make the transition less painful for some individuals.

Today, 50 percent of all first marriages end in divorce, and 65 percent of second marriages end in divorce. Critics say that mounting divorce rates are evidence that human beings are not developmentally up to the responsibilities of marriage. Some complain that marriage is an archaic social form which has outlived its usefulness. In spite of these beliefs, marriage is here to stay; and so is divorce.

Many people believe alcoholism, drug addiction, compulsive gambling, or spouse beating justify ending a marriage. But, today, more people end a marriage simply because the two people in the marriage are no longer the same people as they were when they first married. Simply by virtue of being who they are now, they can no longer satisfy each other's needs.

Jane, after 25 years with one man, says,

"As teenagers, we were in love. We went everywhere

together all through high school. At 19, we married — both virgins; and we had our children by choice.

My husband became an auto mechanic. I took a few night classes, extension courses, summer seminars. After thirteen years, in between children, I had a college degree. I began as a teller and ended as a top executive of a large bank.

At 19, I chose the right man for the person I was and the goals we had. All our dreams of family, home, and travel were fulfilled. It was a good marriage.

When I was 40, we had been together 25 years. I told my husband: 'I love you. I am dying in this marriage. If I am no good for myself, I cannot be good for you or my children. You haven't done anything wrong. I am leaving for my own survival.'

On some level, he understood; but he became extremely bitter and vengeful. I spent two years consumed by guilt. Then he remarried which ended my guilt. Now, he's happily married.

The children, incredibly flexible, live in a world where many of their friends come from divorced families. I trust them to work out, in their own ways, whatever it is they have to work out about our divorce.

I loved our marriage, and now I love being single. All the searching is gone. Although I still love my husband, I never see him. My work, my children and grandchildren, my friends and an active social life fulfill me. I have never wanted to go back."

Harper's magazine polled individuals who had been divorced or separated. Eighty-five percent of the women and 58 percent of the men said they were happier since the separation. Their divorce was a positive action, a turning point in their personal growth. They learned life after divorce was not only possible, but also, in most cases, better than an unhappy marriage. These survivors learned to be resourceful in picking up the pieces and making a new life. They joined the growing ranks of the formerly married.

In a national happiness study, 85,000 Americans answered a questionnaire. The happiest group were **married men**. Married men depend on their wives more than they realize, and they discover that being single isn't as great as they thought it would be. The second happiest group were **single women over fifty**. One woman said, 'Sometimes you have to leave a wonderful, workable marriage in order to grow." Many of these women now remain single out of choice. In general, older women who have been married for years have fulfilled earlier marriage needs. Those women who no longer need financial or emotional support are less dependent on marriage for happiness.

Yet in the process of ending a marriage, you will go through certain definable emotions: pain, shame, anger, guilt, frustration, helplessness, resentment, apathy. In severe cases, you feel like you are bleeding to death.

Eventually, you go through another stage — *Euphoria* — "Free at last." During this stage, you may madly search for the "perfect mate." You are still a true believer, and you want to "try again." You feel compelled to get out every night to find "the right person." To avoid being alone, you join singles organizations. You date a lot of people — some you don't even like. At times, you feel as if you should wear a Scarlet Letter on your chest. But you learn that you are attractive, that people like you for yourself.

Then you find "the man or woman of your dreams." You fall madly in love. At first, that other person is perfect. Then you start seeing the flaws. Little by little the romance wanes. When the relationship ends, you are devastated.

In moments of weakness, like withdrawing from a drug, you want your ex-mate back. You pour yourself into your work, spending many hours on the job.

When that first mad, love affair ends; the disappointment is profound, the pain overwhelming. However, the end of an affair is another beginning. One man said, "Life is never as you used to think it was going to be."

Some divorced people jump from the frying pan into the fire. They get married again within a few years of a divorce. Having lived through one divorce, they now know the process. The next divorce gets even easier.

The painful experience of divorce can result in great understanding and empathy for others who have suffered the same fate. Experiencing the pain that others have experienced can enrich us as we move forward through life.

If you don't remarry, you spend time with yourself, time finding out who you really are at this time in your life. You learn to accept yourself and life as it really exists.

Eventually, you find a new kind of happiness, a peace within yourself. You are no longer driven to find another person to complete yourself. You enjoy your own company as well as the company of others of both sexes. You find a balance of work, family, friends, leisure, relationships — a freedom you never imagined you could enjoy. Reality brings relief and rapture.

The Fractured Family

After a divorce, if there are children, the family does not die. Families live forever. You can divorce a spouse, but you do not divorce your children, even if you never see them again.

During a divorce, you may experience feelings of hatred and vengeance you have never before experienced. You or your spouse may demonstrate unbelievable, bizarre behavior. Two people who once loved each other are now enemies in a war using money and children as ammunition.

She says, "I'm going to push him over the cliff by taking every penny I can."

He says, "I'l fight her tooth and nail. I'm not going to be taken to the cleaners."

In this losing financial war, attorneys often get a large portion of marital assets. No one wins the money battle.

Another way to take each other apart piece by piece is to take away the children — the most feared punishment. You battle over custody of the children.

In fear, she says, "I love my kids more than you do. I'm a better parent. You never spent any time with them anyway."

In pain, he says, "Sure. You brainwash the kids to punish me. You tell them lies about me." Again, everyone — husband, wife, and children — lose; but the children lose the most as they are torn apart by fighting parents.

Today, most courts offer arbitration. In no-fault divorce, the marital assets are divided equally, and judges recommend joint custody of the children. In some divorces, where parents are more interested in the welfare of the children than in vengeance, they work out co-parenting agreements.

Somewhere in a secret place, hidden behind the pain and anger, many husbands and wives continue to love the spouses they left behind — especially those who are the mothers and fathers of their children. With time, many fractured families learn to restructure their lives.

Second Marriages

Statisticians say that by 1990, more married people will be in second marriages than in first ones. Most divorced people remarry

56

within five years of their divorce. But because people who marry a second time are often not prepared for the complications, the divorce rate in second marriages is higher than in first marriages.

A first marriage continues to live — in memory, in body responses, in unconscious emotional places. Unless you have amnesia, you cannot wipe the slate clean. You were married before and that experience becomes the foundation upon which your second marriage is built.

Newly divorced people tend to run on a treadmill. Like a hamster in a cage, you go round and round with "why's" and "because's." You spend hours giving yourself reasons why your marriage ended. "Next time," you think, "I'll do it right." You start searching madly for Mr. or Mrs. Right. You literally do not believe that living as a single person could possibly be a viable option. You have been told that there is something wrong with people who aren't married. They are weird, or no one wants them. You believe you are "nothing" without a spouse. You want to get married again to prove someone wants you.

Men and women who have been previously married are rarely prepared for the realities of a second marriage. They believe they have failed at marriage. The dictionary defines "second" as, "a secondary kind, subordinate, unoriginal, imitative, of inferior position or quality, of less importance than what is first. . . ."

In a survey of 200 second wives, Glynnis Walker, author of *Second Wife, Second Best?*, found, in her survey, these second husbands and wives had known each other an average of two and one-half years before marriage. Slightly more than 75 percent of them had lived together before marrying. Seventy-four percent of the wives worked both before and after their second marriages.

Sex in a Second Marriage

In a survey conducted by *Cosmopolitan* magazine, 46 percent of wives said their sex lives were satisfactory. In a survey of second wives, 86 percent said their sex lives were satisfying. As people get older, their expectations about sex and its place in a marriage change. They know themselves better. Much of the embarrassment about sex disappears. They put less emphasis on orgasm and appreciate the added pleasure of foreplay, cuddling and talking which brings feelings of closeness.

The statistics on infidelity have not changed much for men. Kinsey found, forty years ago, approximately half the men he interviewed had extramarital affairs. But the statistics on infidelity for

57

women have more than doubled. Kinsey reported 25 percent of women, while recent studies show that 54 percent of married women have had one or more sexual experiences outside their marriages.

There is a rise in infidelity with age. Between the ages of 35 and 60, 69 percent of women report extramarital experiences. However, researchers find a decrease in infidelity in the same age group in second marriages. Both men and women have "sown their wild oats," have more experience and knowledge, and fear jeopardizing a second marriage; promiscuity outside of second marriages decreases.

When two formerly married people enter a second marriage, they bring with them issues of ex-spouses, children, money, ex-in-laws, co-workers and friends.

Ex-spouses

In many second marriages, family groups include former spouses, children, and new partners. University of Wisconsin researchers found that over 65 percent of spouses maintained regular contact with former spouses.

Ex-spouses often attempt to hold on to each other using money or children as the reasons. Others want to continue to be good friends. In Glynnis Walker's research, 27 percent of husbands who kept in touch with previous wives said it was "out of guilt." Eight percent said they still saw first wives for sexual reasons. Another 8 percent listed legal or financial reasons. Only 37 percent of husbands had no personal contact with former spouses. Few second spouses are prepared for their mates to be friends with their first spouses.

A much smaller percentage of second spouses face the problem of an ex-spouse who died. The deceased former spouse can make a second spouse feel insecure. A divorce is chosen, but a death can involve the grief of losing a person still loved and wanted. It's difficult to compete with an idealized dead person.

One common confusion is that second spouses often call their new mates by the first mates' names. They make mistakes in dates: anniversaries, birthdays, sizes, and personal preferences. Ex-in-laws also confuse these and other similar items, perhaps not always unconsciously.

Although the majority of husbands in Walker's survey married women who were different from their first wives, 20 percent chose women who were physically similar or who had similar personalities or backgrounds. Fifteen percent of second wives said their husbands tried to change them to be more like their first wives.

Twenty-five percent of the second wives said they felt their husbands, at times, still felt married to their first wives which indicated the ties of a past marriage may be hard to break. Second spouses live with constant reminders that another marriage preceded theirs. What second spouses want from marriage is to be the first priority of their mates in spite of previous marriages.

Children

Many children of divorce live in one-parent families. The parent they live with is responsible to meet their needs and teach them values. The custodian parent is the one who sets the rules: "...pick up your clothes, clean your room, practice the piano, do your homework...No, you can't...."

The irony is that many children begin to long for and idealize the absent parent. Any parent who believes that a child will love them for their sacrifices will learn to swallow the bitter pill of disillusionment.

Each age — infancy, toddler, pre-school, school years, adolescent years — has its unique problems and challenges for the responsible single parent. After children live for awhile with a single parent or in a cooperative co-parenting situation, they learn to readjust. Just about the time a child gets used to this new life, one or both of the biological parents remarry.

Blended Families

In first marriages, a man marries and gains a wife; a woman marries and gains a husband. In second marriages, spouses often marry — not individuals — but families. The shock of instant parenthood with its responsibilities and complexities can be overwhelming to a new spouse who has no children.

If a father has custody of his children, the second woman he marries may not be able to separate his love for her as a person from his need for her as a housekeeper and babysitter. The husband of a working woman trying to support herself and children may not know how much she wants him for himself and how much for help with her financial problems.

In our culture, parents feel their children belong to them. Children are possessions. The birth parents fear they will lose their children's love and be supplanted by a second spouse. Parents are emotionally vested in guarding their children's love. Fear and jealousy toward a new spouse who might win a child's love and loyalty from the biological parent are almost universal.

Children become bonded, in the first few years, to their biological mothers and fathers. Even if a mother or a father is an alcoholic, a child-beater, or a criminal; social workers say young children would rather stay with their real parents than be raised by strangers.

The very existence of step-parents is symbolic of the breakup of the family. The negative feelings children have about stepparents come from such fairytales as Cinderella and Snow White. In both stories the stepmothers are wicked and cruel. Similar stories depict cruel stepfathers. Children often believe second spouses broke up their parents marriage and destroyed their family. However, in general, children are more flexible and more able to adjust to new life situations than are adults.

Blended families of divorce bring more complications because they include ex-spouses, ex-grandparents, and past personal histories. In your second marriage, the wants and needs of you, your spouse, your children and his/her children must be considered. Added to the complications of so many people, hostilities often invade the new family because of the divorce and its aftermath.

Her children will be very covetous of her and everything they consider their territory. His children will be covetous of him and want his attention focused on them rather than on the "intruder." Invariably, children see the new spouse as an invader, the person to blame for their parents' breakup. They will be jealous of their father's or mother's love for the new spouse.

Then there are problems among the children. Unlike the idealized television family — "The Brady Bunch," children of blended families fight for equal time, money, and attention. For example, if his children are teenagers and yours are grade school age, you will need two different sets of rules, two different bedtimes, different demands for food and television programs. No matter how equitable you may be, the children will scream, "Unfair!"

If the children are relatively the same age, they will fight over everything. Children are territorial. They do not like to share toys, rooms, or parents. They do not want to share their parents' time or love with others. But, with luck, after a number of years, the children begin to feel a sense of permanence. In some cases, they even learn to like their stepparents and become friends with the children of their stepparents.

In spite of conflicts, over 65 percent of joint custody parents spend time together as a family unit with their children. Twenty percent of second wives in Walker's survey had children from their first marriage, and 30 percent more wanted children but said they couldn't afford them while their husbands were still paying for children from their previous marriages.

"Yours, Mine, and Ours" was a movie in which a widower and a widow — each with children — married and had children together. Those second wives who want children of their second marriage wonder if they are emotionally or financially capable after being drained by raising children from their previous marriage and the husband's children from his previous marriage.

In some cases, their husbands, already having raised children, do not want to go back and start over. The second wife who persuades her husband to let her have a child of their own, may not have as enthusiastic a father as she would have wished. If the child does not turn out to be healthy, intelligent, or social, the father may blame her.

At some time, you may consider a child of your own from this second marriage. In some cases, depending on their age, children feel more jealousy and resentment toward the "ours" baby. Older children fear that the father will not be able to give them a car, pay for their college education or that he will change his will and leave his money to the new baby. However, in many cases, children from a previous marriage learn to love a new baby — especially if they get a chance to hold the baby, change, feed, and care for it.

With blended families, spouses tend to compare the first wife as mother with the second wife as mother; and first husband as father with second husband as father. Also, both spouses compare his children with her children — as the children compare their real father with their stepfather, and their real mother with their stepmother. Competitive feelings pervade every person in a blended family.

Discipline Problems

Children moving back and forth between two parents often carry messages back and forth — some of which you wish did not get carried. They tell each parent what goes on in the other parent's family. Parents often ask questions and encourage this kind of reporting. Children often learn to pit one parent against the other to get their own way. In blended families, you lose a valued possession — privacy.

Rarely do two different men and women have identical philosophies about how to raise children or how to discipline them. Children raised in separate families have not had the same ground rules for what is considered appropriate behavior by new parents. Adults have many different opinions about what they consider

61

appropriate behavior.
John says,

> *"My wife's first husband, a product of the sixties, believes children should be allowed to develop 'naturally.' His kids take over like savages when they come here. My philosophy is that children need limits and guidelines. When I tell them 'No! You cannot do that in my house.' they get rebellious and 'mouth off." I can't hit them, and I can't change them. I don't want my children to see how they behave or how they talk back to me when I set limits. So I leave when they come to visit.*

Second wives, afraid of being unfair, often overcompensate by being soft with his children which confuses both the children and her husband. Or, in contrast, one second wife who sent a rebellious thirteen-year-old to bed when she was acting up, got into an argument with her husband who said, "She's my daughter, I'll deal with her."

Some children learn to exploit the situation by saying, "You're not my mother (father). You can't tell me what to do."

A united front which includes all four spouses who agree on discipline would provide the ideal environment for disciplining children and make life easier for all — including the children.

There are spouses who lose their right to visit their children. Fighting over children can lead to such extreme behavior as kidnapping. Others voluntarily give up seeing their children because it is too difficult to deal with the constant battles with ex-wives who are jealous of second wives. In such cases, second spouses may quietly blame themselves for taking their husbands away from their family, when, in fact, they had little to do with it.

Sociologist Frank Furstenberg found in his study of children aged eleven to sixteen, only 17 percent had contact with the non-custodial parent on a once-a-week basis. The longer the time since the divorce, the less the contact. After ten years, 64 percent had no contact with their grown children for at least a year.

The Future

Today, divorce rates are up slightly and marriage rates are on the decline. As women become financially independent, one strong motivation for marriage disappears. Also, as more couples decide to remain childless, staying together for the children loses its force for

62

staying married.

In the future, as more children grow up in blended families, more children will experience co-parenting, stepmothers, stepfathers, and being a stepparent themselves. With these experiences, perhaps they will have more empathy and understanding. In any event, marriage, divorce, remarriage, stepparenting, and blended families are here to stay.

Our value systems have changed. Today, you do not have to get married to be "complete." You do not have to have children to live a full life. Getting married and having children are more a choice today than at any other time in our history.

Although divorce, second marriages, and blended families are not without problems, no marriage is easy. All parenting is stressful. Being responsible for children has never been without complications. Marriages end, and children leave. Every event offers a growth experience. *A good life costs.*

5 Sex and Marriage

Underlying the emotion of love is a biological need for contact and closeness with another person.
Alexander Lowen, M.D.

Many of us are aware of the tremendous effects of technology in medicine affecting our sexuality from such extremes as sex-change operations to correcting sexual birth defects. In later years, men and women can turn to technology for such improvements as penile implants. Female eggs can be fertilized in laboratory dishes and implanted in the wombs of infertile women. The high-tech world has invaded our bedrooms.

Along with the new advances in medical technology, many of the old historical issues have yet to be settled. As far back as Adam and Eve, something called "The Battle of the Sexes" has waxed and waned. Is the opposite sex really opposite? Are the differences genetic or social?

What Separates Men From Women?
Tell a couple to look at their nails. Women tend to spread and stretch their fingers, palms outward. Men tend to close and curl their fingers with their palms turned inward.

Tell a couple to look at the bottom of their shoes. Women tend to bend the leg back at the knee and look over their shoulder. Men tend to bend their leg to the side and look straight down.

Watch a couple drinking from a cup or glass. Women frequently look up at the people and the room around them. Men stare down into their drink. This behavior is as prevalent in children as in adults.

Males and females tend to see the world differently. The sexes selectively perceive different elements in identical situations. Women see and discriminate between a much wider array of colors than men. The female brain seems to be more interconnected. Electroencephalograms indicate a greater flow of currents between the two halves of the brain in women.

Women seem to use intuition, men use reason; women are more in tune with Eastern philosophies and religions, men more in tune with Western thought; women look inward and consider their beings, men look outward and make things work; women appreciate music and poetry, men prefer math and mechanics.

The sexes seem to have different talents. Although both sexes can develop any human ability, women are better at combining tasks (hearing what people say while watching body language) while men are better at separating tasks (driving and talking without having one activity affect the other).

Men are also better at jobs that involve components of spatial relations, mazes, picture completion, math and mechanics. Women are better at verbal comprehension, manual dexterity, visual discrimination and language skills.

For women, self-esteem often is based more on personal relationships, but based more on personal performance in men. There is some evidence that women who climb the corporate ladder to reach success find themselves on the analysts couch. One explanation is that women sometimes lose sight of the gender difference — self-esteem, for them, may not come strictly from the visible, material rewards of doing what was thought of as a man's job in a man's world. Generally, most women see softness as strength and feeling as virtue.

During women's liberation there was a tendency to deny that fundamental differences exist between the sexes. Yet 95% of those suffering from anorexia nervosa or bulimia are women. To be different is not necessarily to be inferior. Women are more apt to accept emotions and to openly express their needs. Men tend to be stubborn, resist intervention, and interestingly, to be more dependent later in life.

The old axiom that men use love to gain sex and women use sex to gain love may well fit many relationships in their early stages. However, the sexes are alike in that it's infinitely easier to go from being friends to being lovers than the other way around.

One of the great gaps between husbands and wives is in their notions of emotional intimacy and how important it is in a marriage. For men, simply doing such things as working in the garden or going

66

to a movie with their wives feels like closeness. For wives, intimacy means talking things over, especially about the relationship. Men don't understand what wives want from them. They say, "I want to do things with her, and all she wants to do is talk."

Women want more emotional intimacy while men feel they've fulfilled their obligation to the relationship if they just do their chores. A man says, "I took out the garbage, now let me watch television."

Women who are upset are more apt to talk to another woman, with periods of crying and holding, while men spend the same time running or chopping wood. However, men also go to women more often for advice and support. Both men and women cry over episodes such as arguments, emotional occurrences such as weddings and movies. Flowing tears occur in 47 percent of female crying episodes but only in 29 percent of male episodes, making crying more difficult to observe in men.

Women are more likely to feel, act, then think. Men tend to think, act, then feel.

Carl Jung saw women as estrogen-based creatures and men as testosterone-based creatures. Whereas men have rather specific, genitally-centered climaxes, women experience much more profound, total-being orgasms similar to altered states of consciousness.

Young boys take pride in independence and are threatened by anything that might compromise their autonomy, while young girls tend to experience relationships as part of a network of connections. Boys, as they mature, must learn to connect; girls to separate. Women tend to be uncomfortable with separateness, while men are wary of intimacy. The more comfortable a husband is with intimacy, the more satisfied with the marriage is the wife likely to be.

In courtship, men are more willing to spend time talking to women and to build intimacy. After marriage, and as time goes on, men tend to spend less and less time talking with their wives and more time devoted to their work or with buddies. The trend is strongest in traditional marriages which are still prevalent despite two decades in which these conventional attitudes have been assailed.

A woman can choose to be disappointed, demanding, or unhappy; but she can't force intimacy. Intimacy must arise spontaneously from acknowledging sex differences and through shared activities. The disparities between husbands and wives are part of a wide range of differences that men and women bring to marriage.

Evidence of these differences come from a study of people 17 to 69 years old, some who have been married for as long as 36 years. Men in the study rated as most important in their marriage their

True of Tom?

wives' ability to make love and the couple's shared interests. But the wives listed marital fidelity and ties with family and friends as most important. The husbands said fidelity was more important for wives than for husbands.

The most dramatic difference in evaluating the relationship was that men rated almost everything in their marriage as better than do the wives. Men have a rosier view of love-making, finances, ties with parents, listening to each other, tolerance of flaws and romance. The only thing women rated better than the men was the couple's degree of fidelity.

Marriage researchers are discovering every marriage is actually two marriages; his and hers. Some of the new research suggests that, paradoxically, the differences need not be divisive but can be sources of marital growth if couples will openly acknowledge their differences rather than take them personally.

Do you agree?

The Meaning of Sex

Recent research indicates the three most prominent problems in marriage are conflicts over sex, time, and money. If we were to choose one word to describe what lies behind these problems, the word would be *"POWER"*.

In most relationships, one person has more power than the other. The more powerful person has the capacity to punish or reward the partner. The less powerful person usually has the most to gain by continuing the relationship; therefore, he or she often devises strategies and games for equalizing power.

We learned these games as children when we had less power than our parents. As students, we had less power than teachers. As employees, we have less power than employers. All of our lives we must deal with hierarchy relationships. Although marriage, ideally, should not be a hierarchy relationship, it often is.

In every marriage, brief or interminable power struggles occur. Two domineering people may battle forever, while two anxious, dependent partners may search in each other for the strength and leadership neither can give.

Power need not be equal to be harmonious. A shy, anxious man can find support in an independent, affectionate woman. A dependent, insecure woman may lean on a strong, decisive husband. They chose each other to play these complementary roles.

The balance of power in any reationship is critical. In marriage, the variations of power balance or imbalance may contribute to stability or endless misery. Therefore, awareness of power and how it fits into your marriage is essential.

Sex Role Identification

Sex roles have to do with the way men and women behave or are expected to behave, in day-to-day activities. Traditional, stereotyped sex roles are breaking down. In the past, man was the aggressive breadwinner; woman was the passive homemaker. Man was strong, woman was weak. Man was independent and stoic, while woman was dependent and emotional.

Today, we are beginning to find more differences within the sexes than between them. We now recognize that in each person both male and female qualities exist. More men are getting in touch with their nurturing, tender, dependent selves as women get in touch with their aggressive, independent, competitive qualities. Men can cook, run the vacuum, and change diapers. Women can mow the lawn, fix the car, and be financially independent.

As men and women allow themselves to recognize and develop all sides of their nature, they can choose to let go of the old sex role identifications. Men are not innately logical and emotionally stable, or even independent. Women are not innately flighty, emotionally volatile, or dependent.

Today, it is more socially acceptable for little boys to be passive or aggressive and for little girls to be cooperative or competitive. Boys can be artists, and girls can be baseball players – and both may behave differently at different times in different circumstances, expressing both the classical feminine and masculine qualities.

In a marriage, you can enter a relationship – not according to social sex role identifications – but in relation to your own wishes as well as those of your partner. However, if a woman wants a man who will support her, she will not find happiness in a marriage with a man who wants a self-supporting wife. Similarly, the man who wants a wife to keep house while he works will not be happy with a woman who works long hours as a professional and earns more money than he earns.

Knowing and accepting your partner's personality and characteristics can eliminate problems. For example, if you know your husband is a quiet individual who enjoys reading, the arts, and stamp collecting, you will not expect him to be "Mister Fix-it" who solves electrical and plumbing problems. At the same time, if he knows you dislike housecleaning, he will not expect you to stay home and polish the furniture.

However, needs do change. The same is true of attitudes. A

69

woman who has kept house for ten years may well decide she wants to go to work. A man who has worked for ten years may decide he wants to start his own business or work fewer hours.

Rarely will individual changes in a couple occur in the same direction at the same time. Therefore, communication of feelings and needs is essential. One problem is that changes often precede awareness, therefore, the person who is changing may not recognize his or her own dissatisfactions. A sensitive partner can help the other to recognize changes by noticing non-verbal expressions of resentment, depression, or dissatisfaction.

* * * *

In your journal, write answers to the following to help you find satisfactory roles in your marriage:

1. Think about flexibility and changing roles for a period of time in your marriage to explore how they might work.
2. Write them down. Then visualize scenes in which you play out these new roles. How does it feel?
3. Acknowledge that you need not be consistent — behaving one way or in one role all the time.
4. Share these visions with your partner. Notice your own feelings as you talk about these changes.

* * * *

The risk in changing roles is that you and your partner already have, stated or unstated, agreements about how you will play your part in this marriage. The person who benefits most from past agreements is least likely to welcome change.

Although transitions occur continuously, changes often occur in the form of dissatisfaction that appears in the moment rather than over time. Such changes, when they come to a conscious level, often shock one or both partners.

* * * *

Exploring the following will help you be aware of your transitions:

- Write down what roles you now play in your marriage. (Cook, gardener, housekeeper, auto-keeper. . .)
- What do you like and dislike about these?

- What do you really want to do or be?

Choose a time to share your thoughts with your partner. Is either of you surprised by the differences among your concepts of your roles and your attitudes toward them? If there are gaps between how you live and how you feel, talk about ways to fill in those gaps or ways to make the transitions you want to make. In your journal, take notes of the suggestions that come up during your sharing. Take the attitude of exploration — of changing roles — *not* as a permanent agreement but simply as some aspect of the self that has been submerged and now needs to surface. The writing in the journal is not cast in stone. Neither is the discussion that follows with your spouse. Be open to change.

Sexuality

Although *sex roles* and *sexuality* are closely linked, sexuality refers to the expression of physical love. The last two decades brought with them what the media labeled "Sexual Liberation." We were inundated with thousands of books, magazine articles and television shows devoted to sex. They espoused new attitudes and techniques for lovemaking. The paradox was that as expectations soared, disillusionment increased.

Many books about marital sex give the impression that unresolved sexual problems will inevitably lead to unhappiness and then divorce. According to recent surveys of married couples, many rate their marriages "very happy" even though they say they have less than satisfactory sexual relationships. Such couples are devoted to each other and get along well.

Many companionable, dedicated couples, particularly in the over-fifty age group, in whom impotence makes intercourse infrequent or non-existent, report themselves to be "happily married."

Therapists encounter couples who have "great sex," but whose relationships in general are destructive. In other instances, an excellent sexual adjustment occurs in a mediocre or boring marriage. These couples remind us that sexual adjustment in marriage is only as important as you want to make it and that a good marriage includes many other values.

In spite of all the verbalized changes in attitudes, we have *not* seen much change in sexual expression between partners. People perform sexual intercourse in three basic ways:

1. He does it *to* her (or *she* to him).

71

2. He does it *for* her (or she *for* him).
3. They enjoy sex *with* each other.

Note that #1 and #2 are power positions. The more we depart from the sex object attitudes implied in the first two positions and move toward the equality of the third, the better the physical love-making experience will be for both individuals.

For the last ten years, with the advent of women's liberation and the reevaluation of male/female roles, American attitudes toward sex have been in a state of flux. It's an exciting, confusing time to be alive, especially for those struggling with traditional rules. Attitudes have broadened. Puritanical inhibitions and repression changed to preoccupation with sex. Now, we are moving back toward a more satisfying balance.

Myths About Sex

As we have given up our traditional sex-role stereotypes, we need new methods to achieve a balance of power. However, even in this so-called "age of enlightenment," the old myths of sex continue to thwart genuine lovemaking. In spite of changed attitudes, the following myths persist:

Myth #1 — Men "need" sex.

This myth supposes that a man will suffer physical pain if he doesn't relieve his sexual tension. Although in many young men, semen production builds pressure, this is naturally relieved in nocturnal emissions (wet dreams) or by masturbation. The notion that men "need" sex debases lovemaking to the level of elimination as a body function.

Myth #2 — Sex is a woman's duty to her husband.

The "duty" of sexual intercourse exploits a woman to the function of receptacle for a man's evacuation of semen.

Myth #3 — The man should initiate sexual intercourse.

This myth implies that men are aggressors and women passive receivers. Many marriages have been splintered by the belief that these male/female roles should never change.

Myth #4 — He is responsible for her pleasure and does it to her.

The woman who says, "It's your duty to make me feel good." uses manipulation to avoid taking responsibility for her own pleasure.

72

Myth #5 — He is always, and instantly, ready for sex. True! ☺

If a man doesn't exhibit an instant erection, his mate often
assumes he doesn't love her anymore. Beautiful, tender, physical
lovemaking can be achieved in many ways, even if a man does not
have an erection.

Myth #6 — She is the judge of whether or not he is a good lover.

Destructive women use judgment to castrate men. In an intimate relationship, judging damages intimacy.

*Myth #7 — He is responsible for her orgasm during intercourse,
and/or she is the judge of how long he should last.*

Two words involved in understanding this myth are "responsive" and "responsible." A man and woman can be responsive to each
other's needs at the same time each is responsible for his or her own
orgasm. Every couple can strive for mutual loving rather than judgments of self or other.

Myth #8 — The perfect orgasm should occur simultaneously.

An individual can reach orgasm in various ways. There is no
ideal method or timing. In fact, orgasm is not directly related to
sexual pleasure or satisfaction except in the minds of individuals.
Sexual pleasure is often limited in direct proportion to the narrow
opinions set by either individual.

Myth #9 — All people are monogamous after marriage.

The divorce courts offer ample evidence that this myth is
false. The marriage contract itself does not guarantee monogamy or
fidelity. Utimately, no person can force any other person to abide
by social or personal "rules."

*   *   *   *

Although most of us logically acknowledge that these myths,
as well as others, cause us problems, changing our feelings and attitudes is much more difficult than changing our thinking. Physical
sexual responses and beliefs are less affected by intellectual verbal-
izing than by habitual, long-held attitudinal patterns which resist
change.

Problems With Expectations

It is important to go beyond myths to understand some of the more common areas of sexual expectations, misunderstandings, and disagreements:

(1) Frequency of Sex:
You may want sexual intercourse every day but your partner does not. Do you sulk and fight about it? Do you hide your feelings under a blanket of resentment?

GOOD POLICY

One concept that works for some individuals is to say, "Because I love you and care for you, I am available to you most of the time. Occasionally, I can say 'NO' without it being a punishment or a put-down. You, too, will usually be available to me, and you also may, at times, say 'NO'."

This concept goes beyond being a dull, passive sex receiver. Being available is a choice, not a sacrifice. No one wants a martyr as a sex partner.

Pretense or dishonesty doesn't work either. You can be responsive without pretending ecstasy. To pretend intense pleasure when in fact you find caresses, closeness, security, and touch pleasant sets a trap for the pretender who must continually falsify feelings to be consistent.

(2) Quality of Sex
Anyone who "counts" numbers of orgasms or sexual experiences isn't paying attention to quality. Sex doesn't begin at bedtime with a few minutes of foreplay. Women treasure atmosphere, sensitivity to timing, and a slow build-up with caresses. An atmosphere of intimacy includes continuous, warm feelings between two people. Little moments of thoughtfulness and expressions of attention say, "I love you." Sharing your feelings and sensing when a person is open to touching and hugging illustrate caring.

How does Tom rate here?

(3) Variety in Sex
Some people need less variety in their lives. They want consistency so that they know what to expect. However, we don't eat hamburger and beans every night for dinner.

One of the more common complaints among couples is that they become bored with the habitual ways they make love. Tell your partner you would like to try some new approach, or posture, or different position. However, no one person can demand variety from another. If your partner gets anxious about exploring the unknown, sensitivity and accommodation can alleviate anxiety. Ultimately, if you are bored, you are responsible for your own feelings, and you cannot require that another person take care of your boredom.

74

A change of setting, time, or conditions can create more excitement. Vacations often create a new setting where intimacy occurs more easily. Some individuals successfully fantasize to create excitement. For example, they pretend they are in a different place. They imagine a romantic setting. They role-play, imagining they are someone else — a movie star or actor — in a different place.

If one partner needs more variety than the other, talk out this issue without intending to manipulate but to communicate. If both partners do not freely agree on the sexual exploration, then repugnance can ruin the experience. At the same time, if you have special desires, express them and <u>be willing to have the less adventurous partner set the limits.</u>   OK WITH ME, BUT LET'S DISCUSS "LIMITS"...
AFTER EXPERIMENTING, OKAY?)

(4) Silence and Sex

If you want to be held, you can say so. If you want to be caressed in a special way, tell your partner. Most of us want to please our partners, and we want the other person to verbalize his or her feelings.

Be in touch with your feelings. If you say "NO," be sure that is what you mean. Lovemaking can be like eating. You might say, "I'm really not hungry but I'll prepare a meal for you because I enjoy your pleasure in eating." And it doesn't hurt to talk about the menu. To build excitement, some individuals like to discuss the GOOD details as they make love. Others find talking distracts them from IDEA fully enjoying the sensations. These differences can be discussed at other times rather than at the moment of lovemaking.

(5) Conditions Placed on Sex

Sex is sometimes used as a weapon to get even for something a partner has done. Or some individuals use sex as a bargaining technique: "I will have sex with you if you lose weight. . ." or stop smoking or drinking. To use sex as a punishment-reward device is ultimately a destructive power play.

(6) Orgasm

Many people assume orgasm is a woman's problem and that men achieve orgasm without difficulty. These assumptions lead to sexual difficulties. For the most part, difficulties reaching orgasm are in "the head." Anxiety, fear, and catastrophic expectations interfere with normal, body functions. If we could clear our minds, our bodies would take care of themselves.

Although the conditions under which sex is performed affects a person's ability to reach a sexual climax, each individual is responsible for his or her own orgasm.

If a person thinks it is his or her responsibility to make the partner reach orgasm, this pressure to perform defeats the partner's natural ability to take responsibility for his or her own physical functioning.

Feeling you have failed when you haven't reached orgasm tells you that the problem is in your expectations. The more you feel you have failed, the more likely you will lock into a pattern of failure. The paradox is that the more you let go of expectations, the easier it is to reach orgasm.

The nature and extent of caresses necessary to reach orgasm differ at different times. You can guide your partner's hand to communicate how to give you maximum pleasure. At the same time, openly communicate and help your partner do anything that will help you reach a climax.

I WELCOME THIS; IT HELPS ME GIVE YOU PLEASURE

(6) Erection and/or Premature Ejaculation

It is as common for men not to be able to engage instantly in sexual activity as it is for women. Loss of erection, therefore, should be treated as a normal occurrence. A woman can ask her partner if he wants her to continue to stimulate him or if he would enjoy lying beside her and feeling close.

So-called premature ejaculation is another common problem among men. Again, concern and anxiety are the greatest enemies of satisfactory sex. After a premature ejaculation, a man can continue to stimulate a woman to orgasm. In a half hour or so, they can have sex again.

For the most part, problems in sexual performance come from preconceived notions about what is "supposed" to happen. Any single sexual event cannot be repeated. Each is different. If you accept each experience of physical loving as a new experience without expectations, you can move from making love *to* or *for* a partner to simply expressing your love together.

Intimacy Self-Appraisal

Now that we have discussed sexual myths and problems, it is time to look more closely at your own relationship. Appraise your sexual attitudes and, in your journal, write down how you value sexual relations with your partner. Ask yourself these questions. Then compare your answers with your partner.

1. What does sex mean to me? (Love, closeness, fun, re-

76

lease. . .)

2. What do you think sex means to your partner? (Power, self-validation, intimacy, excitement. . .)
3. In what areas do you believe you are like your partner in terms of sexual wishes and needs?
4. In what areas are you different?
5. What attracted you to your mate?
6. What do you think attracted your mate to you?
7. Recall and write down a couple of sexual experiences with your partner that stand out in your memory as "the best" experiences. Describe them.
8. Recall and write down a couple that you remember as not enjoyable. Do not judge, simply describe.
9. Write a list of things that turn you on sexually. Include time (morning, noon, or night), setting, and situation.
10. Write a list of things you want more of in your sexual encounters.
11. Write a list of things you want less of.
12. In conclusion, write a love letter to your mate.

*   *   *   *

Because each of us is responsible for our own sex life, and abdicate our responsibilities when we expect our mates to "entice" us with techniques, we can learn what to do to get ourselves in the mood for sex. A man who gets turned on visually might enjoy erotic pictures while a woman might get turned on by reading a passionate love story before going to bed. But don't set yourself up by getting ready for sex when your partner may not be in the mood. Being sensitive to your partner's timing and moods is part of your responsibility.

Sexual Relations Inventory
The purpose of this exercise is to assess your sexual relationship. In your journal, write out answers to each of the following:

1. Is your sexual life satisfactory?
2. What, if anything, is missing?
3. What can you do to improve your sex life?
4. What can your partner do to improve your sex life?
5. Can you identify any sexual problems?
6. Who is responsible for your sexual pleasure?

77

7. Do you have orgasms? (Always, sometimes, never)
8. Does your partner have orgasms? (Always. . .never)
9. Who is responsible for your orgasm experience?

From time to time, in every marriage, the sexual experience changes in mood and form as individuals are affected by events outside the marriage. Therefore, when you want more satisfaction, you might find it by reviewing these inventory questions.

In Chapter XII — Marriage Enrichment, you will find more information on sexuality and satisfaction. When sex is integrated into a marriage as a natural part of the partnership, without overemphasis, it will take its role as a satisfying part of loving another human being. Sometimes you will engage in sex primarily because your partner wants it. Sometimes he or she will engage in sex with you because you want it. Sometimes it will not be very exciting. And sometimes, when you least expect it, sex will be so beautiful that it is like a spiritual experience. THIS IS TRUE MORE OFTEN THAN NOT FOR ME!

6 Time and Money in Marriage

Remember that Time is Money
Benjamin Franklin

In our modern world, time and money have become more important in affecting our values. We live life in the fast lane increasingly affected by outside pressures to use time effectively. In every aspect of life, tension and stress are elements of our everyday life. Unmarried people, although pressured by our fast moving world, do not have a spouse to consider in how they use their time and money.

Time is valued, managed, and utilized in different ways by different people. What one person considers a waste of time, another sees as valuable. What is quality time for one person may be viewed as procrastination by another. One person wants a lot of time alone. Another person believes marriage means "togetherness." For greater satisfaction in your marriage, you can learn to balance time: time alone, time with your partner, time with others.

Identify Time Conflicts

In the Western World, we teach our children time categories: past, present, and future. We try to remember what was in the past and anticipate what events will occur in the future. Some cultures do not have language to think about past time. Others do not have a perception of the future. In contrast, we socialize our children to think and talk about the future:

"What are you going to be when you grow up?"

Children as young as five wonder who they will marry and how many children they will have when they grow up. High school students wonder what they should major in to get a job when they graduate, or what college to go to for a degree.

In spite of this cultural orientation, some people are present-oriented and think in terms of "here" and "now," pleasure to experience today. They focus on what they can see or feel in concrete terms. Their behavior is less controlled by punishments and rewards than future-oriented individuals.

A spouse who focuses on the present tends not to plan, organize, set goals or have objectives. Present-oriented persons enjoy present things. They can be fun to be with because they choose immediate gratification — short-term pleasures such as a good meal, an enjoyable relationship, reading for pleasure. Gamblers and drug users tend to be present-oriented. They want experiences "now."

Future-oriented spouses plan ahead, keep appointments, and are usually on time. They value self-discipline, responsibility, and putting off today's pleasures for tomorrow's goals. These individuals are likely to be successful in our technological society where value is placed upon achievement. They save for a rainy day, put money into insurance, plan for retirement. They find less joy in reaching a goal than in working toward one.

Present-oriented people are often attracted to future-oriented ones, and vice versa. When it is time to work, a future-orientation is needed. When it is time to play, to enjoy social relationships and other pleasures, it makes sense to suspend work motivation, daily planning, and goal-seeking.

It is virtually impossible for two people in an intimate relationship to go through life without occasional or frequent conflicts about the use of time. In the first place, each of us has a unique value system. We differ about what kinds of activities are *important*. It is worthwhile to think through our feelings about time.

*   *   *   *

In your journal, write some of your feelings about time as it relates to your marriage. Ask your partner to do the same. Be specific about how you want to spend your time. For example:

- Once a month, I would like to go away with my partner, without the children.
- I would like to have a fixed time for family dinner.

- I would like to have time every day to share the day's happenings with my partner.
- I would like to have some time each day to myself.

After each of you has written your statements alone, compare them and discuss how you can fulfill your time needs while considering your partner's needs.

*   *   *   *

Few of us can be authentic about our real feelings. Sometimes, we don't ask for what we want because we don't know what we want. Another reason we avoid asking for something for ourselves is that we fear conflict. The following are authentic statements:

- Today was a killer at the office. I'd like to have a glass of wine and soak in the tub for half an hour before we share our day's experience with each other.
- I played chauffeur all day and the phone never stopped ringing. I'd like to go into my room for an hour while you watch the kids. Then we can fix dinner.

These statements require a great deal of self-awareness as well as a degree of confidence in your partner. However, if you constantly dream up times to be alone to avoid intimacy or an equal share in the responsibility for running the marriage, then no matter how real your feelings, they will create resentment in the partner if he or she feels cheated of time. Take time to think through what you value so that you will know what you want.

*   *   *   *

In your journal, divide a page into three columns. List the things you and your partner enjoy doing together — Outside the Home, At Home, and On Vacation. Ask your partner to make the same three lists separately from yours:

(1) Outside the Home (movies, lectures, friends. . .)
(2) At Home (talking, music, reading aloud. . .)
(3) On Vacation (touring, backpacking, taking a cruise. . .)

Now make another list of things you enjoy doing alone. Compare your lists with your partner and discuss changes.

*   *   *   *

Over the span of a thirty-year marriage, some men and women give up the things they have wanted to do all their lives. One woman said, "My husband would never travel with me." One man said, "All my life I wanted to go camping in the wilderness, but my wife simply could not stand 'roughing it'."

These statements could illustrate a game Eric Berne calls: "If it weren't for him (her). . ." which people use to avoid feared activities. In these two cases, these individuals played "martyr." The net result is buried longing or resentment for not fulfilling their own needs. She played "Good Wife" and he played "Good Guy" at their own expense. Their resentment is self-chosen. They could have chosen to fulfill their own needs.

In *The Virtue of Selfishness*, Ayn Rand says that any person who does not fulfill his own deepest needs will not be any good for anyone around him. Those spouses who continuously over the years give up what they want for spouses or children often believe they are being self-sacrificing. When these people become filled with longing, resentment, or frustration, they sometimes silently punish those around them.

Resolve Time Problems

If time management problems revolved only around you and your partner and children, solutions would be relatively simple. However, friends, extended family members (parents, siblings) and significant others fulfill certain needs in our lives. In addition, how each of us spends our time is related to those things or experiences that we value most. Many decisions we make about how to spend our time are intricately connected with money — what things or experiences cost.

Time spent at work affects marital interaction and family relationships. Work patterns can destroy a marriage. If one person works a considerable distance from home, transportation time cuts into family time. If husband and wife work different schedules, they have less time together.

In some cases, work is a divisive force in American marriages; it can block communication, destroy intimacy, and leave little time for relationships. When work seems unnecessary in terms of meeting the true economic needs of a family, it may meet other needs. No one can give you a value system. Through communication, a married couple can reach a better understanding about values and time. If

82

you want to be married, some degree of negotiation is essential to meet the needs of both spouses.

Time Management

The most important concept about "Time Management," is that first you *must* know what you value so that you can manage to satisfy your priorities. Then you can communicate with your partner and share with him or her the importance of how you want to spend your life.

Use your journals. Begin by making a chart with the following headings:

1-Estimated   2-Reality   3-Wanted

1. How I think I usually spend my week (estimate work time, transportation, sleep, eating/dressing, family time, etc.)
2. Keep a chart for one week of how you *actually* do spend your time.
3. Now compare your estimate in #1 with the reality in #2. Most people are surprised by the discrepancies between how they imagine they spend time and the reality.
4. Finally, write how you would really like to spend your time.

Compare your lists with your partner's. Set a time to discuss time issues and negotiate a schedule that allows time for family communication and intimacy. These lists will change as your interests and values change. Once a need is fulfilled, it disappears and new needs take its place. Being conscious of these changes can be developed.

To take control of your time is to take control of your life. Understanding how to make choices will help you avoid time conflicts. You are a *Decision Maker*. You are responsible for whether you are happy or not.

If you have difficulty making decisions, then recognize this problem and work on it. Once you can make decisions, you can start to plan, to set priorities, and to move toward your goals. Planning can be for this day, this week, this month, or this year. Long-range plans, such as buying a house, take many years. If you make a choice, you are responsible for changing that decision when it no longer fulfills your needs.

You can run into problems if you are inflexible, unwilling to change when new information tells you to set new goals or move in another direction.

We all have the same amount of time. Using that time effectively means selecting those tasks from all those available and doing it the best way you can. To become a more effective spouse or parent or worker means doing what works to reach your goals. Too much organizing and planning can be as undesirable as too little.

Time Priorities

The purpose of this exercise is to assess your goals, to order your priorities, and to look at your use of time.

A. Both partners should answer the following questions in writing without consulting each other.
   1. What are your goals for next year? (Be specific. Think of work, family, school, money, etc.)
   2. What are the three things you most want to accomplish during the next year?
   3. What obstacles block your management of time?
   4. What are your biggest problems in managing time?
   5. Does your partner have problems in managing time?
   6. What goals for the next year do you think you share with your partner? For the next ten years?
   7. How can your partner help you achieve your goals?
   8. How can you help your partner achieve his/her goals?

B. Discussion: Compare your answers with your partner's. Spend some time clarifying ways you can help each other reach personal as well as joint goals.

The use of time is highly personal, a matter of individual choices. Different techniques work for different individuals. Ultimately, however, time control is a matter of greater freedom in your life.

Life is a never-ending process of choices. Today, technology gives us more possibilities than at any other time in history. These choices are often complex and difficult. Some people prefer not to choose. But not choosing is making a choice not to choose. Then you are responsible for the results of not choosing. We want someone else to decide so that if their choices don't bring us satisfaction, we can blame them. It's difficult to take responsibility for our choices. But, in the end, we are responsible for our own satisfactions and dissatisfactions with our lives.

If you often choose what you think others want you to do — a parent, a boss, or a spouse — you may resent it or you might feel good about pleasing the other person. But you are the one choosing, for whatever reason, to do the pleasing.

Finally, our choices change as our situations and roles change. A spouse will choose one behavior with the other spouse and choose a different behavior with a child or with an employer. Choosing is difficult. We have so many things we want which we cannot have — at least not in the moment. We must balance short-term goals and long-term projects to reach the goal that is most important to us.

We are mortal. Our lifetime is limited. How we spend it is critical. Assuming that marriage is high on your list of values, you will want to resolve time conflicts and manage time in cooperation with your spouse to enrich your marriage.

Money Management

Close friends discuss the intimate details of their sex lives but avoid the topic of salary. Celebrities flaunt their wealth with diamonds and flashy cars but won't tell on television how much they earn. The subject of money is more secretive than sex or delicate than death.

According to researchers, surveys indicate married couples fight more over money than sex or time. Money is intimately connected with our value systems and often linked with power. Often the person in a marriage who controls the money has the power. Sometimes money is used as a substitute for love when one person tries to buy another's loyalty or affection.

In a capitalistic society, money is connected to self-value. Comparing salaries is one way people measure their worth. Many people believe a baseball player who earns $1 million is more valuable than a social worker who earns $20,000.

We measure a person's worth in direct proportion to how much money he or she earns. Often we assess our own self-worth in terms of how much money we make in comparison to others. Therefore, non-wage earning housewives — even though they have important responsibilities for mothering, household work, and volunteering — often feel defensive about their value.

In our culture, money is a taboo subject. Since we can't talk about money, we try to prove how much we are worth by buying objects such as expensive cars, houses, or furniture that become symbols of our value.

When one partner becomes overwhelmed with a need to prove

self-value by spending money, he or she becomes self-indulgent. The 'Madison Avenue" mentality pushes some individuals to acquire more than they need to prove to others – with the acquisition of possessions – that they have worth.

The other partner, in self-defense, often sets up spending restrictions. Then the couple plays child-parent games: a restrictive parent and a rebellious child.

In other cases, the power struggle becomes, "What I Want" *vs.* "What you Want": my fur coat against your new car. If I give up my fur coat and you buy the new car, I can play martyr or punish you. However, I have a choice. I might feel good about our joint decision to buy the car now and the coat later or vice versa. First, I satisfy one of your needs and then I get what I want next time.

One spouse prefers spending money on experiences such as travel or education, while the other wants to buy "things." This difference in values must be negotiated.

If one partner wants to accumulate objects while the other partner needs the security of a retirement account, these differences in money values can be the force that drives them apart. One wants immediate gratification while the other wants to plan for the future. Time and money are intimately connected.

For millions of people, inflation and income loss are serious threats to household and personal security. Even the wealthiest families suffer when investments "go wrong" and the future is uncertain.

When Wives Earn More Than Their Husbands
Although the majority of husbands earn more than their wives, some wives today are receiving attractive, lucrative job offers with large salary increases. Many husbands now find themselves making compromises that wives used to make.

Today, more American families are tossing tradition to the winds and putting wives in the role of primary breadwinner. The 1980 Census Bureau shows there are 5.9 million families – 12 percent of all U. S. couples – in which women earn more than their husbands. In 4 million of these families, both the husband and wife work, while in 1.9 million, only the woman is a wage earner.

Contrary to popular thinking, most of these women are not "superstars" with executive jobs. They often perform less glamorous work to make up for a spouse who is unemployed or working part-time.

86

According to the census report:

- Thirty-six percent of wives in such families hold professional or managerial jobs; 38 percent have finished more years of school than their husbands.
- Fifty-five percent do not have children at home.
- The median income of such households is $23,547 — substantially less than that of families in which the husband earns more than the spouse but slightly higher than families in which the husband is the sole wage earner.

Although some researchers say that marital unhappiness is a side effect when women earn more money than their mates, happiness may be in "the eye of the beholder."

Cathy Carter has always earned more money than her husband. She loves running on the corporate fast track, earning $48,000 annually, while her husband, Carl, prefers a more relaxed pace in a $16,000 a year job with an electrical firm. Carl, 37, who graduated from the University of California, says, "It's a philosophical position for me. I'd feel uncomfortable making megabucks, especially if she were making them too."

Carl, who was a Peace Corps volunteer, puts personal relationships and learning new things ahead of job status, money and advancement. He says, "I want to make a comfortable living, but 80-hour work-weeks and tension and pressure are not for me."

Cathy describes herself as ambitious. She says,

"My ego needs more feeding than Carl's. If I were earning less than my husband, I'd be jealous and in constant competition to see who got the bigger bonus or most raises. I'm lucky to be married to Carl. He doesn't feel threatened, challenged or inadequate because I earn more than he does."

This couple has worked out their financial partnership. Both contribute to their expenses in proportion to their earnings. The money each has left over is spent, saved, or invested as each sees fit.

As for household chores, they are performed by agreement. Cathy hates to do the bathroom, so Carl cleans it. Cathy cooks because she enjoys it. Carl says, "Basically, we just pitch in."

Each two-income family has problems to be worked out. Scott's friends kidded him because his wife made twice as much as he did. Mary, a television reporter, earns $75,000 a year while Scott makes $30,000 as an editor. At first, the disparity put strains on their relationship. Mary didn't like putting up most of the down payment on their residence.

"My part seemed out of proportion," Mary said. It hurt more to use all her savings because she had woked hard and saved money when she was only making $8,000 a year.

At first, Scott and Mary set up separate checking accounts in addition to a joint account. Ultimately, the process of trying to allocate funds between joint and personal accounts proved confusing and conflicting. Eventually, they closed their personal accounts. These transitions are evidence of the changes in a relationship.

Over time, Scott and Mary learned to live with income disparity. Mary says, "If you love each other, you work it out just like you do any other problem. There's no magic in that."

Irrational Money Decisions

Most people make economic decisions in irrational ways. For example, a sizeable percentage of incomes are spent on alcohol, tobacco, deodorants, cosmetics and endless substances that are useless or harmful.

While some people lack adequate housing, they spend their money on cigarettes. Narcotics are used much more by the poor than the well-to-do. People who cannot afford basic foods buy shampoos, hair tints, and cosmetics. Others who can't afford medical care buy tickets to football games. Families who do not give their children adequate educations buy cars. Economic problems are, in the final analysis, psychological problems.

Our economy pushes people into buying more than they actually need. Few people wait until they can pay cash. The debt games, using credit and loans, can destroy individuals and families as well as governments.

We have become a society of people constantly in debt and always wanting more – on both a personal and social level. Like puppets, pushed by fear, competition, and insecurity, many people allow money to run their lives.

Identify Money Problems

Money is often more of a taboo topic than sex. It is tied to issues of greed and competition as well as aggression and possessiveness. Money symbolizes a number of different things to different people.

Read the following list and make a list of what money means to you. Make a list of what you think money means to your partner.

- Power
- Possession and control
- Security
- Substitute for love
- Independence and freedom
- Status and recognition

Take the time to delve further, to determine what money means to you. Write the following statements on paper and rate yourself on a scale of one to three.

1-rarely   2-moderately   3-often

1.   I buy things I do not need.
2.   I use money as a source of power
3.   I use money to control my spouse
4.   I use money to feel secure
5.   I use money as a substitute for love
6.   I use money for prestige — to look good to others
7.   I use money for "the good life" — clothes, cars, jewelry. . .
8.   I use money for travel, vacations, experiences. . .
9.   I use money to convince myself I'm important

Compare your responses with your partner. What are the differences?

Negotiate Money Conflicts

As we have emphasized throughout the book, negotiation and compromise work best for most people in areas of conflict, including money. Value systems differ. One partner may feel the need to save money for future security while the other partner believes in using money for the good life. One partner may enjoy shopping while the other one hates it. Some couples argue over two incomes, particularly in those cases where one income is considerably greater than the other. These value differences must be negotiated.

At the end of each month, many American couples have spent all their income, yet they have no idea where it has gone. The first step is to sit down together and write down your income and your expenses.

In some marriages, both partners agree that one person manages money better than the other. So one partner takes control of the management. But both partners make decisions about how the money is spent, and both partners can be aware of money decisions.

In every marriage, a couple should have a will stating how they want the assets distributed in event of a death. Every couple who cares about their future should have a financial plan and keep it updated.

Insurance, pensions, social security, and other realities need to be discussed. The process of reaching joint decisions and compromise can add satisfaction in a marriage.

We have considered the role of power in marital relationships. Sex, time and money are often used to manipulate a spouse. Although a certain amount of manipulation occurs in most marriages, power manipulations can cause suffering.

In the best marriages, couples develop harmonious balances of power so that both spouses have their preferences met. When you get something you want, you will then want something else. That's what life is about — getting what you want, recognizing changing preferences, and moving toward new goals.

Subtle, minor power maneuvering occurs in many marriages and is within normal limits. Ultimately, every married couple can negotiate their differences in the areas of sex, time, and money.

7 Children and Friends in Marriage

Children begin by loving their parents;
After a time they judge them;
Rarely if ever do they forgive them.
                                        Oscar Wilde

As adults, our technological world has crept up on us. Our children were born into it. Computers in the classrooms, satellites above the earth, and space vehicles for transportation are facts of daily life taken for granted.

Most of the time, we also tend to take our relationships for granted. However, if you had to move from your childhood home, change schools, or leave a job where you liked the people you worked with, you have had an experience of how important family, friends, co-workers, or neighbors can be to you.

Most of us want to nourish and be nourished by many persons. The desire to be with others varies from person to person. It also changes within a person from one stage of life to the next.

As children, we need a nurturing person to love and encourage us as we change and grow. As adolescents, our social life outside the family becomes more important to us as we develop friendships. The next stage is marked by mating relationships which are sometimes followed by a desire for children. For most of our lives, we continue to relate to other people.

Relationships have a beginning, a middle, and an end. Beginnings are often exciting, chaotic, or beautiful. As our relationships change, we sometimes live through transitions unaware of those changes. At other times, when a relationship grows, we experience little moments of rebirth. As a relationship dies, we experience little moments of death.

Today, we acknowledge time and energy limitations. We cannot be all things to all people at the same time. We must order our priorities in relationships.

Kinds of relationship not only have great individual variation but also often overlap. Because they are not mutually exclusive, several kinds of relationship needs can be satisfied simultaneously. We can enjoy spousal and parental relationships at the same time we enjoy friendships and community connections.

Children

Our most vital human relationship is the bonded love between parent and child. Only a generation ago, having a family was considered a natural consequence of marriage. However, in the 1960's, when the birth-control pill became widely available, family planning advocates began an extensive education program. Americans became concerned about over-population. As a result, "Zero Population Growth" became the battle cry of the 1960's.

In the 1970's, liberal laws relating to abortion brought a whole new way of thinking about having children. Today, some young couples, for a variety of reasons, do not want children. Some couples want only one child. Others plan on two or three.

Whether or not to have children is one of the most important, long-lasting decisions a couple will make.

If you decide to buy a house, you can change your mind and sell it at any time. If you decide to have a child, you have made a twenty year legal, social, and moral commitment. After that time, your parent/child responsibilities will change legally, but your bonds last longer than the lifespans of two generations. A death ends a life, but the parent/child bond lives on in the survivor.

John, 35 years old, married Linda who had a seven-year-old daughter by a previous marriage. They have been married five years. Linda says,

> *"If John wants a baby, I would be willing to have one. I think he would make a great father. But he can't make up his mind. This is one decision I won't make for him. It's irreversible."*

Today, as men are freed from the responsibility of earning the total family income, they are expected to share more responsibilities for the family at home. However, when the question arises as to how spouses will juggle career and family commitments, working out this balancing act is still primarily a woman's problem.

Who Is Responsible For the Children?

Although husbands are glad to have two incomes, they expect the woman to be responsible for the children. To explore your own expectations as a couple, answer the following questions:

1. Who will change and wash the baby's diapers?
2. Who will get up in the night with the crying baby/child?
3. Who will make the formula?
4. Who will stay home with a sick child?

We hear talk about "Super-Mom," but we don't hear about "Super-Dad." Although more men think about these problems than they did a decade ago, it will be interesting to see how these issues will evolve in the next ten years.

Why Do Some People Want Children?

If you want to evaluate whether or not you want to become parents, both husband and wife can use pencil and paper to answer the following questions. This exercise will help you come to a clearer decision about family planning. (If you already have children, answer the questions as honestly as you can.)

Whatever your motivations for having children are or were, your answers will give you information about yourself and your expectations for your children. There are no "right" or "wrong" answers. Conceivably, you could answer "YES" to every question.

1. Do I want a child to prove my adulthood — to prove my masculinity or feminity?
2. Do I hope to experience through a child things that were denied to me as a child?
3. Am I trying to achieve, through a child, things I failed to achieve?
4. Am I trying to save a shaky marriage by having a child?
5. Do I want a child as an outlet for affection?
6. Am I conforming to traditional expectations that a couple should raise a family?
7. Am I trying to fulfill a maternal/paternal "instinct"?
8. Do I want children so I can stay "young in spirit"?

9. Do I hope to mold a child who will be the smartest, prettiest, best dressed, or best athlete on the block?
10. Do I want children for my old age or to carry on the "family name" or to give me "immortality"?

Whatever your reasons, many people see having a child as a means to an end which ultimately can interfere with enjoying the child as a person. From time to time, continue your discussions about wanting or not wanting children.

A women can answer the following questions:

1. If I want children, how many? How far apart?
2. Is a career more important to me than having a child?
3. Can I handle a satisfying career and still have time and energy left to raise a family?
4. Do I want to go to school first, or do I want to have a child first?
5. If I decide to have a child in mid-career, how long would I be willing to stay home with the baby?
6. What kinds of childcare arrangements will I make?

A man can answer the following questions:

1. If I want children, how many? How far apart?
2. Can I handle the financial and emotional drain of a child?
3. Am I willing to participate in the daily care of a child?
4. Does my job require a lot of time away from home?
5. How do I feel about my wife going back to work and leaving my child in the care of other people?
6. Would I be willing to put off a career to raise a child?

The answers you write today will change next year. Change is the one constant in our lives. We cannot be sure that our mates will stand by the answers they wrote yesterday.

However, when the two of you compare your answers to the preceding questions and discuss them, you will have a better understanding of each other's feelings about having children.

Past circumstances may surface. For example, a person who remembers a mother's near-death in childbirth may be afraid to have children. A person from a large family will either resent all those brothers and sisters or wish to have a large family of his or her own to repeat the earlier pattern.

Examine your attitudes toward children. Search for the hidden past experiences and emotions that guide your decisions. To clarify your values, write answers to the following questions:

1. Why do I want children?
2. What are my expectations from them?
3. What are my goals for them?
4. How much am I willing to give of myself?
5. Am I willing to give up material comforts for them?
6. Am I willing to give up my personal freedom for them?

Wanting and having children involves deep feelings and complex, hidden motives you may never uncover. Wanting a child may be as basic as wanting your mate's genes to join with yours. More simply, it may be a desire to see and hold the fruit of your love-making. Can you say the following?

1. We enjoy children.
2. We are financially able to support children.
3. We are willing to spend the time to raise children.
4. We have enough energy to raise children.
5. We have enough love to give to our children.

After all the soul-searching and writing, wanting a child is a powerful drive that, like an instinct, takes over. All the planning, talking, and analyzing will not prepare you for parenthood. Ultimately, raising a child is a frustrating, frightening, and joyous experience.

The moment of giving birth — or bringing forth a life — can be experienced by both mother and father. Bonding with a child begins at the moment of birth for those who want the experience. A wanted child is, for many, the fulfillment of life.

Fictions About the Family

The perfect family may be one of the most insidious fictions in America today. Family life rarely goes smoothly. A Confucian proverb states:

"No family can hang out a sign saying, 'No problems here'."

- Children get sick.
- Children fight with each other.

95

- Children get angry and throw temper tantrums.
- Children manipulate parents and siblings.
- Children get jealous of a parent or a sibling.
- Children are torn by sibling rivalry at the same time they experience love/affection/loyalty for one another.
- Children need chauffeur service to doctors, dentists, school, friends homes, music and swimming lessons.

The list is endless. Often the demands are set by the parent on him or herself. If you want your child to be academically successful, excellent in sports, drama, and music, these expectations you set will rarely be met.

The cost in disappointment is high. We are so image conscious in our country, we set goals our children cannot meet. The danger is that you must protect yourself from yourself, or you can end up feeling totally swallowed up by your parenting demands.

Agreements, Commitments, and Contracts

Children learn the value of an agreement through family interactions. When we love someone, we want to say "YES" to their every demand. However, parents must learn to say "NO" a dozen times a day. Often one parent becomes the "NO" parent while the other covertly acts in collusion with a child.

For example, David and Jane had a son twelve years after their daughter was born. David identified with the son and found it difficult to say "NO" to anything he wanted. Jane became the strict disciplinarian who tried to instill in the boy all the lessons she had learned through mistakes with her daughter.

After several years of confronting their difficulties, David admitted it was not a loving act to give the boy everything he wanted. At the same time, Jane realized she was overly strict to compensate for David's failure to give their son direction and discipline. David, Jane, and the son sat down together and wrote down some major agreements in the form of a contract.

One part of the contract dealt with money — how much to give and for what purposes. They agreed on certain rules and time limits. The three of them periodically reviewed their contract. As the son demonstrated that he was able to handle more responsibility for his own behavior, they amended the contract.

Every parent must deal with pain and disappointment. Children seldom follow the pathways we envision for them. Ideally, most parents would like their child to be an "A" student who excels in sports and is "President of the Class." In a world that measures success in terms of academic, financial, and social success, it is difficult not to want our children to excel in everything.

Many parents view their children as extensions of themselves. If a child has difficulty in school, in sports, in making friends, we tend to take it personally — as if we have failed as parents. These feelings war against our reasoning powers when we acknowledge that our hopes or demands for our children's success are unrealistic.

Brune Bettelheim, Freudian psychoanalyst, says that American parents tend to set unreasonable expectations for themselves, their mates, and their children. He suggests that despite college educations, many parents are unable to accept either the idea or reality of dealing with a difficult child. The relationship between parents and children has never been put under so many pressures as it has in our "fast-lane", Hi-Tech world of the last twenty-five years. Technology appears, if anything, to complicate the task of raising children.

Letting Go

As children grow up, parents face new problems. As teens, children want more freedom from parental standards, at the same time they make more financial demands. Most teens want to drive a car — preferably their own — and experiment with alcohol, drugs, and sex. As their adolescents move into the adult world, parents often feel threatened by the damage children can do to themselves and others. Parental responsibilities for children from twelve to eighteen are at their heaviest.

Letting go is a gradual process and depends upon how well the child follows safety rules and moral conduct. Unfortunately, many children must learn life's hard lessons by being hurt. Caring parents seldom find that ideal line between being over-protective and over-permissive. Even within a family, the lines are different for different children. Therefore, success with one child does not guarantee success with the next one.

A common middle-age crisis occurs for both men and women when the children leave. We can prepare for this transition.

*   *   *   *

In your journal, write answers to the following questions:

1.   How do I feel about being alone again with my partner?
2.   How do I feel about our years ahead, together?

3. What kinds of relations do we want with our grown children?
4. What do I want to do with my life now?
5. What do we want to do with our time together?

The "empty nest" clears the path to creative retirement — time to develop talents such as painting, writing, or woodworking — time to relax and cultivate new friendships.

Friendships

Many people want friends. Yet a good friendship must be nurtured. The cost in time, energy, and thoughtfulness is high. As a result, friendships can be a source of dissension in a marriage. Because friends may either interfere with or enrich a marriage, you can ask yourself, "Do I really want friends?"

The word *friend* is one of those imprecise words that conveys different meanings to different people — or even to the same person at different times. Friends do not fit into boxes but more on a line — a continuum that goes from an acquaintance — someone we recognize and converse with — to someone with whom we enjoy intimate sharing.

Write down names of people under the following categories. (Feel free to make up your own categories.)

Acquaintances   **Our Friends**   **My Friends**   **My Best Friend**

From this list, begin to develop a definition of the word *Friend* and what it means to you. For example, describe a "friend":

- a person who supports me and is uncritical
- a person who is reliable, loyal, trustworthy
- a person who accepts me as I am
- a person I respect and feel safe with

Or you might want a friend:

- who can help me find my own self-deceptions
- who trusts me enough to tell me how he or she really sees me
- who I don't have to handle with "kid gloves" for fear he/she will feel hurt.

98

- who I can get angry with without losing him or her

It's important to most of us to be with people who we *really* enjoy being with. When we first meet a new person who seems to enjoy our company, the conversation is animated and exciting. However, over a period of time, we may find that the conversation lags — or even worse, gets boring.

After a few weeks, Frances found herself politely listening when Linda's conversation was filled with superficial, meaningless verbiage. Then Francies found herself increasingly irritated. She had always disliked trite conversations. Meaningful communication was too important to her to tolerate Linda's small talk — her dialogue about trivial events of the day, her experiences with people Frances hardly knew, her intolerable requests for favors.

Frances preferred one good friend to several superficial relationships. Frances could confront Linda by sharing her feelings, but she felt that Linda was happy with her level of relating and needed friends who would relate in a similar way. Because telling Linda might hurt her, Frances withdrew from her relationship with Linda by introducing Linda to a woman with compatible social needs.

Friendship Boundaries

We have difficulty coming to terms with the transitory nature of human ties. However, the attempt to involve oneself fully with too many people leads to self-destruction and emotional emptiness. We must choose certain friendships to nourish and cultivate. Some independent individuals are relatively self-contained. Deep, involved friendships are not as vital in their lives as their families or their work.

If you want friends, you must allow time to cultivate them. You must set a schedule of how often to meet — taking into account their needs as well. If it is enough for you to meet with a friend four times a year while she feels she would like to see you once a month, you must work out this discrepancy. The time you choose to spend time with others and how you spend that time are your decisions.

In your journal, write answers to the following questions:

1. How often do I wish to entertain at home?
2. How often do I want to go out with friends as a couple?
3. How much time do I want to spend alone with one friend?
4. How do I want to spend my time with that friend?

If you are a growing, changing person, your answers to these questions will change. The number and kinds of relationships you want when you are twenty-five will differ from those when you are forty-five.

No matter how fulfilling any friendship, certain needs will remain unfulfilled. If you are aware of the rewards as well as the costs of friendship, you will find that what you want from a friend changes over time.

Friendships Change

The average family in the United States moves every five years. People change jobs even more often. Although we live in an age of rapidly changing values, we do not want our friends to change.

One way people change and grow is to move on, to make new friends more suitable to their next level of development. To be aware of personal and social changes is a lifelong goal.

We learn about friendship through direct, inexplicit experience as well as by explicit awareness. However, we have difficulty when a person changes. Change is so gradual — we can't see it or feel it. It can't be measured. Yet we must deal with change in our friendships.

The opportunity to change is one of the most exciting possibilities in life. However, most of us want our friends to stay the way they are and not change. We are threatened by change. Trouble arises when changes test a relationship. If change goes beyond the tolerance level of the other, then the friendship can become spotted with criticism and bickering.

Some endings occur when two friends slowly drift apart. If a change produces an abrupt withdrawal by either person, it may feel like rejection or betrayal. "I liked him and trusted him and now look what he has done to me."

The ideal friendship includes trust. Trust is a state of mutual reciprocal interest in which we allow the other person the freedom to change — to actualize his or her potential.

Since we become more of what we potentially can be in relationships with others, through friendships we grow as human beings. Although we want to be giving — selfless, caring people, we must search for a balance between self-concern and concern for loved ones.

Friendships End

Pain and grief often accompany the death of an intimate friend-

100

ship. Few of us know how to handle endings. We feel guilty if we do the leaving and betrayal if we are left. Most of us feel we have failed if our friendships do not last "forever."

Friendships include certain consequences — the unfreedom of people bound together in relationships. For any friendship implies mutual demands and expectations. The more intimately involved a friendship, the greater the pressure each person exerts on the other to fulfill expectations.

The danger is the imprisonment of past values, a return to a time when individuals were more tightly bound to one another and were also more tightly regimented by social conventions.

Many people today have come to terms with the transitory nature of human ties in a fast-moving, urban world. Although friendships may be limited in time, they need not be superficial. Length of time has little to do with a quality of friendship.

We can enjoy medium-duration relationships with friends, neighbors, job associates, as well as with co-members of churches and clubs. We can also enjoy short-duration acquaintances with our auto mechanic and hairdresser. At times, certain relationships turn out to be more enduring than those with neighbors — like one with a family doctor. Today, the average friendship is shorter in duration than in the past.

As we become more proficient at making new friends, leave-taking and breaking away become easier. However, separation does not necessarily end a relationship. We often maintain contact with one or two friends from the old location if only through our yearly Christmas card rituals.

Stability based on close friendships with a few people is affected by high mobility, wide interest ranges, and varying capacity for adaptation and change. Some individuals will continue to value "old friends" while others will develop the ability to form and then to drop friendships quickly. They will form many more friendships and their friendship patterns will provide them with different forms of satisfaction.

More people today are substituting many close relationships of shorter duration for the few long-term friendships of the past. Ultimately, each of us chooses the numbers, kinds, and durations of our friendships.

We make a mistake when we treat our spouses, children, and friends as if they are possessions that belong to us. We feel as if others often perceive us as objects, to be known and used. We see each other as status symbols — professional, physically desirable, wealthy.

101

We approve or disapprove of others in terms of whether they satisfy our needs. According to Freud, almost every intimate personal relation leaves a sediment of aversion and hostility because we use each other as objects that administer pleasure and pain.

With our hostility, we feel shame. We experience guilt as we find ourselves in the marketplace of human relationships — of achievement and success measured by who relates to us. Shame can be transcended when we acknowledge that love and aversion, closeness and distance, pleasure and pain depend upon their opposites for existence.

A Sense of Community

A basic need of every human being is to belong, to be part of something larger than himself. To belong and to be needed is to feel important, to have a basis for self-esteem and inner security. We have many spheres of life: family, friends, work. Through a sense of community, we find these aspects of our life become unified and integrated. George Bernard Shaw said,

". . .my life belongs to the whole community, and as long as I live it is my privilege to do for it whatever I can."

In the past, personal meaning for an individual's life was supplied in the context of a coherent community. Tradition prescribed patterns of relationships within a culture. Those born into a society were set upon a stage with a predestined part to play.

Today, we can't count on pre-defined roles. Each of us must build meaning into our own lives and build it through our commitments — to a family, a religion, an ethical order, a life's work, or to fellow human beings.

Personal obligations in your life exist because of what you have to offer. Each of us has the privilege and the duty to contribute to public service even if it involves nothing more than performing superbly whatever tasks we set out to do. Each of us has the power to make a difference in the society in which we live.

Each person creates meaning in his or her own life through commitments to others. Viktor Frankl said, "The meaning which a being has to fulfill is something beyond himself. It is never just himself."

Some people run around searching for their personal identity, but they will never find it "out there." A person finds identity through commitments to others. Again, we face a balancing act —

that changing, amorphous balance between self-concern and social concern. For, ultimately, we can only give what overflows from our own fulfillment.

The great issues of life are too complicated to be reduced to some simplified formula. Those who boil down every issue to some ideology or doctrine often become righteous but rarely solve social problems.

Social Responsibility

A democracy is not only a political but a social expression of the values of freedom and equality. Each of us, to the limit of our capabilities, takes responsibility not only for our own actions but also for the society in general. This value emphasizes a service orientation, helping others, giving of one's self, a concern for the public interest in contrast to narrow self-interest.

A lot of disappointed people have wanted to change the world. If we accept the world in all its complexity, then by working on some small corner of a single problem, we can sometimes be involved in some modest improvement. Each of us sets our personal and social goals. One goal can be to make life less difficult for others — child, spouse, friend, or neighbor.

Albert Einstein said, "Only a life lived for others is a life worthwhile." It's a magnificent experience in life whenever we can do something to make our world a bit better.

Some individuals develop a sense of community through neighborhood programs. Some volunteer a few hours each week to work with young children. Others specialize in gerontology — the fastest growing segment of our population — people over 65 years. The old, the disabled, and the helpless in our society provide us with opportunities to make a contribution. Some people work with national or international social organizations like the United Way or The Hunger Project. Five million Americans, from New York to Los Angeles, joined hands across our country to demonstrate that they were united against hunger and poverty.

On a community level, every problem we solve creates another problem. Modern science has cut the mortality rate and prolonged the human lifespan with the result that we have a population problem. We replace manual labor with sophisticated machines and automation with the result that unemployment grows.

As efficiency becomes more important, work is dehumanized. As affluence grows, we have greater per-person waste. Increasing wealth results in growing disparity between haves and have-nots.

Each of us can choose from the many social problems, some small corner in which to work for change.

In a large part, we create our world of relationships. As children, we usually spontaneously give and take warmth and affection. We enjoy hugs and kisses and being held. We expect parents to give us emotional and financial support as well as protection from the outside world. As adults, we find more fulfillment in a spirit of giving to something bigger than one's self and without expectation of material reward.

A Giving Society

Philanthropy comes very close to the concept of a giving society. Its Greek root means literally "love of mankind." The giving society not only gives financial assistance but time and personal concern for the welfare of others. Thousands of non-profit organization, such as Scouts, colleges, churches, hospitals, libraries, and non-profit organizations are made up of individuals willing to give of themselves.

Nearly 150 years ago, the Young Frenchman, Alexis de Tocqueville, when he visited the United States, said:

> *These Americans are the most peculiar people. . .a citizen may conceive of some need which is not being met . . .He goes across the street and discusses it with his neighbor. . . .A committee comes into existence and. . .begins functioning on behalf of that need. . .All this is done by the private citizens on their own initiative.*

The paradox is that we also value capitalism as an economic way of life. Some of this economic exchange system spills over into our personal relationships.

We cannot be close unless we can be distant. All-perfect love does not exist. To learn to love as humans, we must separate the unrealities of sentimentality and idealism. The all-perfect marriage, the perfect parent-love, the ideal friendship, the all-perfect humanitarian — these are myths, neither possible nor desirable.

However, the paradox is that the more caring we express, the more we experience in return — like electrical energy that comes from us out to others and then back to us in an energy circuit. For love is the overflow of our own fulfillment that we give to others — to children, to friends, and to the community.

8 Creative Communication

*Once a human being has arrived on this earth, communi-
cation is the largest single factor determining what. . .
happens to him in this world. . .*

Virginia Satir

The most important element of any sound relationship is communication. This flat statement sounds trite, but it describes reality.

Profound wisdom must be learned over and over and over. The
willingness to learn over and over and over something we are convinced we already know is the mark of a wise person.

Most of us believe that we *are* communicating all the time —
with other people as well as with our partner. The fact is that we
habitually *tell* things to others and sometimes listen half-heartedly
when they tell us something. Much of our communication is often
superficial and empty.

We hear what we want to hear or make assumptions about what
the other person is saying rather than hear what is said or what the
other person intends to say. We lock into past evaluations and
emotional responses about the person speaking that prevents hearing
the real messages.

The word *communication* itself is abstract and few of us talk
about what we mean when we use the word. It originally came from
the idea of *community*, of *communing* with another person. It
means more than simply discussing the weather or world affairs. It
implies a degree of depth and intimacy.

The essential point you want to reach in a marriage is the
ability to express to a partner what you *need*, what you *feel*, and
how you feel about him or her. And it is important to be able to

105

express yourself without damaging the other person's self-esteem.

As babies, we communicate our wants by crying when hungry and laughing when happy. But as children we are told "don't cry" or "don't be silly." We soon learn to hide our feelings rather than reveal them. We are also taught what is socially acceptable to talk about and what is not. Emotions are often *not* acceptable — especially for men.

At the same time that you censor what you say, you unconsciously communicate nonverbally through your body language: tone of voice, facial expression, body posture and gestures. When body messages conflict with verbal messages, you send "mixed messages" which confuse others.

However, as speaker, you tend to believe what you say and deny what you feel. This self-deception results in your losing consciousness of your feelings. As a result, you often do not know what you really want.

As a human, blessed with speech, you have the ability to relearn how to clearly communicate your wants if you know what they are. But after years of censoring and saying what you believe is expected — what is socially acceptable, you often have difficulty sorting out what you want from what you think you "ought" to want.

Therefore, to communicate clearly, you first have to become conscious of what you want from your partner. Then you must be willing to develop your verbal skills so that you can risk asking for what you want. This is a very complex process.

It takes courage to ask for what you want because the other person can say "NO." At times you may choose not to risk. However, having made that decision, you can no longer blame the other person for not understanding who you are or what you want. Clear communication has a price and not everyone is willing to pay the cost.

Steps in Effective Communication
1. Know Yourself:
If you decide to hide your feelings or needs from others, you may lose awareness of them. Certain techniques will help you get in touch with what you want. Although many of your fantasies may be impossible to achieve, by freely exploring them you can learn more about yourself than you now know. You can hold silent dialogues with different aspects of yourself. By listening to what each facet of your personality feels and says, you can get in touch with parts of

yourself that you do not display in your relationships.

For example, do you secretly yearn for a fancy sportscar that you can drive with the top down, wind blowing in your face, free from all worries and cares? Or do you secretly yearn for a cabin in the mountains with a simple, earthy lifestyle instead of living in your crowded apartment with the noise and bustle of the city?

Or do you imagine yourself free of clothing on the beach basking in the sun, free from the constraints of the world? Do you like your body? Have you recently looked at it closely?

If you want to know yourself better, remove your clothes and study yourself in the mirror. Without making any judgments, look at your face and hair, your neck, shoulders and chest, your thighs, legs and feet. Feel the texture of your skin. Touch your genital organs. Get to know your body.

Notice your feelings. What parts of your body do you like? What parts do you wish were different?

At this point, you are simply getting to know yourself as you are.

Sheryl, a lovely, young woman, married only three years, found herself getting fat. At first she was not aware of her compulsive eating, but as her clothes got tighter, she had to buy new ones. Then she began to step on the scale every morning.

Sheryl's husband used to compliment her on her appearance. Now the compliments ceased. Although he did not make any negative comments about her weight, he complained about the bills for clothes as she bought increasingly larger sizes.

When Sheryl passed 150 pounds, she cried. She said to herself, "I've got to do something. I hate my body."

In essence, Sheryl was no longer the physical person she had once been and wanted to be again. By thinking through her problem honestly, without rationalizing or excusing herself, she came to realize that she was using rich, heavy food to compensate for something that was missing.

After a few months of marriage, her husband had gradually stopped telling her how beautiful she was. By eating to compensate for this loss (rather than being able to tell him her need), Sheryl was not only indulging a need for gratification but also, subconsciously, punishing her husband for his lack of attention. The entire process occurred unconsciously.

For her own satisfaction and to regain her husband's admiration, Sheryl went on a diet. In two months, she lost fifteen pounds. One evening her husband said, "You look lovely this evening."

This reward more than compensated for her self-denial in food, but Sheryl's greatest reward was an awareness of who she was, what she wanted to look like. By communicating with herself first, she was able to gain for herself and from her husband what she needed.

Another way to become more aware of yourself is to keep a journal. Mark a section of your workbook as your diary. Each day — or as often as seems comfortable — write ideas, thoughts, needs, desires, fantasies. These entries can be stepping stones in getting to know your feelings by expressing them.

Sherod Miller and his co-authors in *Alive and Aware* give a simple way to answer the question "Who am I?" You are a different person at different times. You are the thinking you, the feeling, wanting, doing, and sensing you.

Miller presents an awareness model which tells us we can increase our awareness of five dimensions: wanting, sensing, doing, feeling, and thinking.

*   *   *   *

Ask yourself exactly what you're experiencing at any particular moment. Practice this awareness model until you become more conscious of what you want, sense, do, feel, and think:

1. What am I sensing? (Sounds, sights, odors, temperature, etc.)
2. What am I feeling? (Anxious, satisfied, bored, angry, etc.)
3. What am I thinking? (Evaluations about yourself/spouse, etc.)
4. What am I wanting? (From myself, my spouse, others)
5. What am I doing? (Actions to get what I want, asking, etc.)

*   *   *   *

In your journal, jot down key words or briefly summarize your thoughts, feelings, and actions as a method to find out more about yourself and what you really want. Pay attention to all aspects of yourself. As you repeat this exercise over and over, you will be surprised how much more you will learn about yourself.

Some individuals take time from the chaos of daily living to tend their own gardens — to nurture their beliefs, opinions, ideas, expectations — those critical personal parts of us that affect our marriages.

Often you communicate nonverbally through posture, body movement, voice intonations, facial expressions, gestures, and physical distance from the person with whom you're communicating. You may think you are communicating one message while your partner is actually receiving something entirely different.

One way to become more aware of body language is to notice your facial expression when you tell someone you're angry. If your jaw is clinched and your eyes narrowed, the tone of your voice will sound harsh. Your hands may be clinched.

At another time, if you're smiling and laughing, and you try to say the same words, your tone of voice will sound like you are kidding. Your partner will not know how to take what you are saying.

Have you had someone jokingly say something cutting with a smile? Then if you get angry, that person says, "Can't you take a joke?" Those who use teasing and sarcasm habitually are often unaware of buried hostility and anger from the past. Out of habit, they get used to hurting others. The words say one thing; the smirk says another. Out of habitual behavior patterns, many of us give such mixed messages.

More commonly, when one person is trying to hide emotions such as anxiety, the verbal and body language are at odds. For example, Harry, whose wife has been ill several times, is often anxious about her health. She, in turn, is unhappy that she troubles him. As a result, she often resents his repeated queries about her health. Harry says,

Over the years, I've learned not to press the point because she doesn't like me hovering over her like a mother hen. When she is closed, cold and remote, I worry that she is irritated by something I have done. She will insist nothing is wrong, but her tone of voice and facial expressions tell me otherwise.

When you deny your feelings and say what you think another person wants to hear, there will be a discrepancy between your spoken message and body message. It is important to express yourself clearly, honestly, and directly.

Assert Yourself
Learning what you want to say is only part of communicating. You can learn to like and respect yourself — and what you have to say — rather than trying to say what you think others want to hear. If you do not make sure your partner understands clearly and directly what you need, you stand little chance of having your needs

109

met in your marriage.

Asserting yourself does not mean to be arrogant or belligerent. It does not mean that you can demand from any other person that they meet your needs. It simply means that by communicating your desires, both you and your mate will know what they are. Hiding your needs sometimes happens out of habit. But, more often, it occurs because you fear rejection.

To open and share yourself, to take a chance by trusting your partner not to take advantage of your vulnerabilities, you pave the way for better communication and greater intimacy.

Helen, whose husband has a college degree and status in the community, felt inferior. She had to go to work after high school graduation. Because of her lack of a college education, she feels embarrassed to join her husband at social gatherings where everyone has more education than she has. Helen is convinced that if the discussion gets on an intellectual level, she won't have anything to contribute. Helen tells this story:

> One night we were going out, but I dreaded it. I can't honestly say that I had ever been put down by Dick's friends, but I always felt that sometime I would say something dumb that would embarrass him. That night I dawdled longer than usual at the dressing table, unable to get myself ready.
>
> Dick got so exasperated he yelled at me. I burst into tears. He took me into his arms and asked me what was wrong. The words just spilled out. . .about my feelings of intellectual inferiority and embarrassment. Dick was amazed. He said he had no idea I had been laboring under this burden of concern and uneasiness all these years.
>
> He called our host and said we couldn't come. We spent the evening in comfortable clothes, curled up together, sipping a bottle of wine, and talked the whole thing out.
>
> As we talked, Dick assured me that never once had he been embarrassed by me. In fact, he thought I always held up my end of any conversation. He said, 'A college education doesn't guarantee a person will have any common sense at all, or that they will be clever or wise.' Dick said he valued me for my common sense and practical knowledge.
>
> I never loved Dick more than I did that night. We would never have reached such a beautiful level of inti-

macy if I hadn't opened up and told him my fears. As a special bonus, I now have more confidence when we spend those 'intellectual' evenings with his friends. I have lost my imagined feelings of inferiority.

Listen with Empathy

One part of effective communication is opening up and revealing your needs, fears, and desires to your partner. Another important part is to really *listen* and *hear* what the other person has to say.

It is difficult to open up, to trust, to be vulnerable. To be effective requires that another person concentrate on both your verbal and body language, to listen and understand the meanings behind the words.

And beyond understanding is empathy, that state of comprehension where a person can say,

> *Darling, I understand what you're trying to say, and I can almost feel the way you are feeling. I feel close to you when you trust me this way and I will not betray that trust.*

When you learn to listen and are willing to give and receive feedback, you are usually rewarded with the most important, private information by another person. This kind of intimacy is rare and to be treasured as one of our goals in communicating.

Think about how much of the communication between you and your wife or husband is judgmental. How often do you hear or speak judgments: "Can't you ever keep this house cleaned up?" or "Why do you always come home late when you know I have dinner ready at six?"

These "you" questions are not really questions at all. They are statements of blame. We judge our partners for something they have done that displeases us, and then make them wrong. The problem is judgments don't work to change behavior.

Use "I" Statements

To avoid this kind of communication and improve your relationship, use "I" statements. You can tell your partner how his actions affect you and how you feel without playing blame-games or trying to put blame on the other person. For example:

111

1. Avoid "You" blaming: "You make me angry when you . . ." Rather say, "I feel angry when you. . ." Take responsibility for your own feelings without blaming others.
2. Avoid interrogation:

   "Where were you last night? It was past midnight when you got home, wasn't it?"

   Such an accusatory interrogation immediately puts the other person on the defensive. Instead say,

   "I was really worried last night when you didn't get home by nine as you said. I realize that at times it's difficult for you to break away, but I would appreciate a call if you see you are going to be late."
3. Avoid general, vague pronouns. Sometimes we use "it," "we," or "they" to attribute our own feelings to some other source. For example, "Women (they) want their husbands to. . .." Instead say, "I wish you would. . . ."

These and other speech habits are part of our cultural programming. They interfere with effective communication. Each of us must speak for ourselves, using "I" messages, and accepting responsibility for expressing our own feelings.

Exercises in Communication
Following is a series of exercises designed to help raise your level of awareness in communicating.

Silence as a form of communication has many meanings:

- Silence can express closeness and intimacy.
- Silence can express anger and tension.
- Silence can be a withdrawal into separateness
- Silence can express dislike or wanting distance.
- Silence can be used to shut out or punish another person.

The following exercise can help you become more aware of how you use silence. Sit facing each other, without speaking, and look into each other's eyes. Start with thirty seconds, then one minute, and finally two minutes. Afterward, share your thoughts and feelings during the silent period with your partner.

In the future, when you are both silent, be aware that *you are communicating*. Get in touch with your interpretation of that silence. Write it down. Get some feedback from your partner about

112

the meaning of that silence to him or her. Discuss your feelings to find out the meaning of silence to your partner and to share your feelings about silence. Learn to listen to silences as well as to words.

Communicate Through Your Body

Your body communicates continuously. It has its own powerful language. Whether you use words or not, your body communicates independently. Words transmit your messages on one level, while your body involuntarily reveals your thoughts, feelings, and attitudes on another. These messages are demonstrated by the way you move, sit, stand, and by your gestures and facial expressions. Be aware of this form of communication. Learn to observe, respond to and listen to your own body, so you'll know what it is saying to your mate, and what his or her body is communicating as well.

As a test, before you and your partner go to your next social affair, agree to check out with each other your own and his or her *real* mode during certain times of the evening.

For example, if your partner seems to be listening to a joke that his boss is telling, but has a forced smile and is facing partly away from his boss as if trying to find an escape, check with him shortly after. Was he really interested in what his boss was saying, or was the boss telling a joke he's told many times before? You'll learn to be more sensitive to body cues as you practice.

Closeness or Distance

Sit near your partner while you talk to him or her about something personal. Then move away about three feet and try to find a comfortable distance between you. Move closer again — six inches apart — and make eye contact. How does it feel now?

Your body has a "safety" zone; if another person invades your private territory, you feel tense and restless. You need to move away. Each person's zone is different with different people. There isn't any right or wrong amount of space. Comfort or discomfort differs with each person's own sense of safety.

Next, turn your backs to each other, facing in opposite directions and tell each other something personal. How does it feel to talk about an intimate subject without eye contact?

Finally, hold hands while you talk and look into each other's eyes. Touch each other another way, and then say the same thing without touching and without eye contact. Do you notice a difference? Share your experience with your partner. You're learning how much space each partner needs to communicate effectively.

In the communication process, each of us relates on two levels. One level is *content*, the meaning of the words that are said. The second level is *process*, the feelings that are conveyed with the words. Feelings are conveyed by tone of voice, facial gestures, posture, or timing.

For example, a wife tells her husband she's depressed because of an unpleasant incident at work. He comments, "That's too bad," but continues to read his newspaper. Reading the paper indicates disinterest in her problem while answering perfunctorily. The two levels of communication — content and process — are *incongruent*. They do not match; they are inconsistent. For clear communication, the process and content need to match to be congruent and consistent.

Speak for Yourself

This exercise gives you the opportunity to practice the "I" statements we discussed earlier. Begin all your remarks with "I" rather than "we" or "you". For example, when you say, "We always like to be together," you are speaking for another person. Your togetherness will be demonstrated by sharing, helping, and doing things for and with each other. When you wish to express your opinions or feelings, don't talk for your partner.

Sometimes while saying goodbye to a host, one person will say, "We had a very good time." Speaking for the other person is artificial. You may do it out of habit. When you break your old communication habits and begin to think about how you communicate, the process will improve and be more authentic.

Questions to ask yourself:
1. Who makes most of the decisions? Is that okay?
2. Do you feel free to assert yourself and to say "No"?
3. Are you threatened by your partner?

Role Reversal

In order to facilitate empathy, you need to get into the other person's "shoes," to feel his or her feelings, to see a problem from the other person's point of view. Complain about something that bothers you and let your partner respond spontaneously. Now exchange roles. Let him repeat your complaining so you can hear it from his point of view. Keep in mind that there are many positions to see, understand, and resolve with any problem.

It is a mistake to assume that good communication is simple.

114

When you take all the variables into consideration, it is a tremendously complex process. Many of us believe we are communicating effectively when, in fact, we are not. How do we know?

Ask for Feedback

Check with the person you're trying to reach. Another indicator of effectiveness is whether or not you are getting what you want. The problem may be that you do not know what you want; therefore, you cannot ask for what you want. Or if you ask, you ask in such an obscure way that the other person cannot give you what you want even if he or she wishes to do so.

Here are some questions to ask yourself and each other to evaluate your communication skills:

1. Do you express your thoughts clearly?
2. Do you really say what you want to say?
3. Do you often use superfluous words or repeat to get your messages across.
4. Do you use too few words, leave gaps, or make assumptions, in stating your position?
5. Do you skip around haphazardly, or stick to one subject before going on to the next?
6. Do you spend time clarifying your meanings if your partner says he or she doesn't understand?
7. Are you being congruent (consistent in words and body language) in what you communicate?

Evaluate Your Communication Skills

Write answers to the following questions:

1. Much of the time do you really listen to and hear what your partner says or do your thoughts wander?
2. Do you question your partner when you do not understand?
3. Can you allow differing opinions or do you try to persuade your partner to see everything your way.
4. Do you listen *completely* to what your partner says or do you form your response before he or she is finished talking?
5. Do you often interrupt before your partner has finished statements?

These questions simply call to your attention some problems in

115

listening. If you notice something to work on, you can practice those parts of your communicating skills that need work. One excellent method for really listening is to repeat your partner's statements.

For example, if he says,

"I feel that our sex life is unsatisfying, and I think we should do something about it."

You restate:

"I hear you saying that you don't enjoy our sexual relations and that we should work to improve them. I'm willing to talk about it. Give me some specific examples of what you don't like and make some suggestions about what changes you want, and I'll do the same.

You've agreed to continue the dialogue. Each person can restate his or her position before moving on to solutions. However, not all problems can be solved. Because each of us is an individual attempting to live with others, we must live with conflicting needs.

A choice that confronts all of us every moment is whether we want to open ourselves to be known as we are. We can choose to remain hidden. We can wish to be seen as someone we are not. We can pretend to feel differently than we do. Viktor Frankl says, "No one can become fully aware of the very essence of another human being unless he loves him."

People who feel they are worthy of love can usually accept love and give it. Caring is a process. It is a way of relating to ourselves and to someone else. Caring involves time, trust, and a willingness to allow the person — self or other — to grow.

Milton Mayeroff, in is book, *On Caring*, lists seven major ingredients of caring: knowing, patience, honesty, trust, humility, hope, and courage. He says, we cannot care for everyone. To care for another, we must know them.

Relationship is a process of self-revelation in which you discover your own motives, your own thoughts, your own values. This discovery process is the beginning of liberation, the beginning of transformation. Communicating who you are includes the messages you send with your body, with your words, and with your actions.

Creative communication is a goal, not a place that is ever reached with perfection. You and your partner can practice the skills of creative communication and conflict resolution from this

116

book. The communication skills you develop can contribute to a better marriage relationship.

People need each other to help resolve conflicts, clarify values, and find out about themselves. The gifts of listening and responding are gifts we give each other to show that we care and are cared about.

There is evidence that humanity is now on the threshhold of vast new possibilities. We have just begun our consciousness evolution. We are in the process of moving beyond our present state of communicating and relating.

9 Conflict Resolution and Negotiations

He who lives without conflict is a bachelor.
Saint Jerome

Some of the patterns by which we shape our lives grow out of biological differences. Interestingly, opposites attract. A bright-eyed morning person marries a nightowl. An independent person who needs alone time marries a dependent person who needs lots of togetherness. A logical-thinking person marries a sensory-feeling person. An introvert marries an extrovert.

These opposites are attracted to each other's differences before they decide to spend every day for the rest of their lives living together. Then, when they live together, they cannot understand how their spouses can possibly view the world in such diverse ways.

Other sources of divergent values between spouses is rooted in family backgrounds. The values of parents, teachers, and friends affect them differently. Even birth order affects personalities. When two oldest siblings marry, they are both used to being the responsible, decision caretakers of the family. When two youngest siblings marry, they are both used to getting their way and being babied. Middle children, bossed by older siblings and passed by for the "babies", have special needs for lots of attention to make up for what they didn't get.

Family of origin also includes a social and economic class, a religion, a community, a life-view. Thus biology, personality differences, family and community values, and dissimilar environments result in unmeasurable marital conflicts.

The Value of Conflict

You can learn how to live with, accept, confront, and negotiate personality and value differences. Good communication skills do not prevent conflict. Intimacy leads inevitably to conflict situations. You cannot maintain a level of intimacy without occasional disagreements. If you believe you have an intimate relationship, but say, "John and I never argue; we never fight," then chances are your relationship is not *intimate*.

One reason you may believe it is always right to "keep the peace" and never engage in upsetting confrontations is that society places a high value on this condition. Only in the last decade or so have some people begun to question the value that peace is best at any price.

Dr. George Bach, author of *The Intimate Enemy: Creative Aggression*, has conducted considerable research on constructive conflict. He says, "Couples who fight together are couples who stay together — *provided they know how to fight properly.*"

Bach describes fighting unfairly or dirty as "gunny-sacking" which describes two partners who accummulate and hide their grievances. Then a trivial incident will be sufficient for one or both to explode and haul out all the old hurts and angers they have stored. Typically, in this kind of unfair fight, partners try to hurt each other by attacking vulnerable points.

If a couple has been close, each knows all too well how to hurt the other. A woman who wants to hurt an insecure husband attacks his masculinity. He might retaliate by calling her a bitch. She escalates the situation by accusing him of being a poor provider. Then he counterattacks by accusing her of poor housekeeping, and so on, *ad infinitum*. Obviously, a few seconds of this kind of fighting obscures the original subject.

To prevent gunny-sacking, keep all arguments fair and current. Set aside some prime time on a regular basis to air your grievances. Couples who fight *regularly* and *constructively* don't need to carry gunny-sacks full of complaints or bring past grievances into every argument.

Fights fall into a consistent and repetitive pattern. Most couples fight about the same things. They may use different words, but their behavior and reactions are predictable.

Not all fighting is verbal. Passive rebellion comes in many forms. For example, you can get back at your mate by forgetting something important, misplacing the mail, forgetting to pay bills, or in some other ways acting irresponsible.

Now, using your workbook, remember and summarize your big

and little fights of the past. What is the common denominator among them?

For example, a man might repeatedly complain about cobwebs, dust, and dirt in the house. His wife may be irritated by his failure to shave or hang up his clothes on weekends. Although these are not major conflicts, these minor irritations fill up a bucket with drops until the bucket overflows.

Write down the things that irritate you. Place them in order of priority. Choose one item to discuss. Without demanding that your partner change, tell him or her about this irritation. Do not discuss it. Simply share it.

When you let trivial annoyances accumulate uncommunicated, they can grow like yeast – all out of proportion. However, you cannot expect the other person to change his personality. If you voice your complaints, you get them expressed. But you cannot manipulate another person or force them to please you.

The Value of a Productive Confrontation

Several things can be accomplished:

1.   Feelings are expressed.
2.   Each person lets the other know what his feelings are.
3.   Each gains new knowledge about the other and about situations that involves them both.
4.   A level of renewed or deeper intimacy can be reached.
5.   A workable compromise or solution can be found.

If a confrontation feels like a fight in which one partner feels like a winner and the other feels like a loser, you have both lost. The pompous winner ends up with a resentful loser. However, if both partners feel they have gained something – such as the relief of expressing feelings – then the sharing was productive.

Ultimately, the goal is to practice negotiating skills – even for the smallest disagreements – such as whether to eat out tonight or stay home. Negotiating on small disagreements helps develop skills for large ones.

Fighting as Catharsis

Some couples fight simply to release tension. In this type of fight, the two are not requesting change from each other. There is nothing to win or lose. The topic and form of this fight may be the same time and time again. This ritualistic encounter, Bach labels a "round robin." It goes nowhere and the antagonists wind up at an impasse. If tension release is what they're seeking and an impasse is where they want to be, this "game" works for them. However, if they wish to move beyond impasse, Bach suggests three steps:

1. Agree to a moratorium on all repetitive fighting.
2. Introduce a specific change so that the cause of the fight cannot happen again. (For example, a wife may complain that they sleep all day Sunday because they go to bed too late on Saturday night. They might agree to go to bed earlier and get up earlier every other Sunday.)
3. Determine the real reason for repetitive fights. (In the above example, the wife really wanted to make love on Sunday morning instead of sleeping. Her real complaint was that her husband was not giving her enough attention.)

Keeping Distance

At times, one function of a fair fight is that of regulating the emotional distance between two partners. After being together a great deal, one or both feels a need for separation. One person may set up a fight to justify more space.

A close relationship challenges that delicate balance between intimacy and suffocation. Each partner has different needs for closeness and distance. You need to leave each other space to grow without so much separation that the intimate quality of the relationship is endangered.

Gerald Smith and Alice Phillips point out in *Me, You and Us:*

"If a 'coming together" is the essence of true closeness, it follows that this cannot be achieved without occasional distance."

Couples who have too much togetherness and intimacy are advised to take a short vacation from marriage. Each can go away alone for a few days or at least spend a day or an evening apart. Usually, both partners will feel refreshed, renewed, and more intimate when they are reunited.

To recapitulate, here are some of the principles involved in a "fair fight":

1. Observe your partner's vulnerabilities and respect them.

(Do not attack to destroy.)
2. Stick to the real issues. (Am I angry at my husband for spending too much money on the children or because he refused to let my buy new carpeting?)
3. Choose a good time for the fight. (Do not pounce when your partner is down.)
4. Level with your partner. (Be honest about your feelings and the issue of disagreement.)
5. Get feedback from your partner. (Listen actively, send "I" messages, confirm what you have heard, and work together toward a solution.)

The fair fight is an open confrontation in which both partners are straight, open, and equal. Both listen openly, not defensively. Each genuinely wants to know what the other needs and requests.

Avoiding confrontation often leads to *emotional divorce*. Often we avoid confrontation because we were taught that aggression, conflict, and anger are unacceptable — taboo. Nice, intelligent people, we were told, do not raise their voices in anger. Yet, we cannot stress often enough that partners who do not fight do *not* have an intimate relationship.

In a dead marriage, no one fights or disagrees, because no one cares enough. In an honest, vital relationship, fighting serves a definite function and has its place.

Obviously, no one wants to be near an angry partner who is out of control, who yells and screams. You have the right *not* to respond to a shouting person who attempts to manipulate you through aggression. However, if you regularly avoid arguments because you are afraid to bring up a subject, your marriage is in trouble.

Here are some of the ways we avoid confrontation:

1. Hide behind a newspaper or television.
2. Ignore what your partner is saying or remain silent.
3. Fall asleep. ("I'm too tired to discuss it.")
4. Develop a headache or stomachache.
5. Change the subject.
6. Delay the issue. ("Let's talk about it later.")
7. Give something else a higher priority. ("The children need me." Or "The lawn needs to be mowed.")
8. Communicate through body language, "Leave me alone."
9. Accommodate by saying "yes" to end the discussion.
10. Discuss trivial things to avoid any real issues.

None of these is a permanent solution for avoiding conflict. They may work temporarily, but then you reach a point where you must deal with your differences or resentment turns into indifference. Then you find yourself in an emotional vacuum.

Total conflict avoidance leads to a "dead marriage" where partners relate to each other in a light, superficial, inconsequential manner. They do not level with each other, and they do not confront. Their typical conversation goes like this:

She: How was your day, darling?
He: Fine, thank you. How was yours?
She: Okay. Do you want a drink before dinner?
He. Good idea. I'll have my usual on the rocks.
She: Strong or weak?
He: It doesn't matter.
She: What do you want to do tonight?
He: Whatever you wish.
She: You know I don't care as long as you're happy.

In this nice, peaceful home, nothing more meaningful is said all evening. Their discussion continues with:

Shall we watch TV?
Do you want the newspaper?
I think I'll go to bed now.
Goodnight, dear.

The next day is just as lovely, peaceful, and empty. These people cut themselves off from creative communication. They have trained themselves never to disagree. Emotionally they live in separate houses.

"The Accommodator"
Accommodation is that state in which a husband or wife agrees with any situation or discussion in order to avoid friction. The accommodator may never get anything he or she wants. Following is an example of accommodation:

She: My sister and her children will come to visit this summer for a month. Won't that be fantastic?
He: (Looks angry but says) Yes, dear. That will be fine. (He thinks, "I hate those brats. There's never a minute's peace while they're here. But I can't stand

124

hassling her, so I'll shut up.)

His resentment builds because he refuses to confront his wife. He thinks his wife ought to know what he is feeling. He assumes she can guess what he wants; therefore, he thinks she is deliberately making him miserable.

We often make the mistake that our partner can read our minds or guess what we want. We need to check out our assumptions and express our feelings.

"The Nice Guy"

The always-agreeable person — and many of them are women — has been trained to shun anger as a bad thing and encouraged to be 'nice" all the time. This kind of behavior is unrealistic. The "nice guy" is afraid to:

Express anger
Be assertive
Be rejected
Confront directly
Deal with conflict

He or she is afraid of not being loved. Such a person believes being agreeable and avoiding conflict is the way to be loved. This person is afraid his/her negative feelings are ugly, thus hides them. As a result, such a person:

1. Alienates the self from the partner by keeping a distance.
2. Feels resentment and fear.
3. Represses frustration until it explodes.
4. Eventually leaves the marriage physically or emotionally.

If either partner in a marriage is a nice guy, the marriage will be virtually meaningless. Being married to a "nice guy" leaves the partner feeling empty. A partner can tell his/her mate that he/she feels hollow; and that intimacy in a relationship means that sometimes they must disagree. It is okay to confront each other with differences.

The Silent Treatment

The final form of conflict avoidance that we will discuss is passive-aggressive behavior — the silent treatment. Two partners who are angry but afraid to express it may pretend everything is alright. They avoid honest confrontation through silence. For example:

> *She: Dear, I waited two hours for dinner. Finally, I ate alone. (Thinks, "I'm angry, you bastard. You never come home on time. You don't care about me at all.")*
>
> *He: That's okay, darling, as long as you ate a good meal. (Thinks, "I work hard all day and what does she do? Why can't she at least wait and serve me a warm dinner, the bitch!") He picks up the newspaper and ignores her.*
>
> *She: (Feeling left-out) Darling, I want to tell you about my mother. She called today. (She waits for a response but gets silence.) "Darling, mother is sick and needs my help. I told her I would ask you first, but if it's alright, I'll go see her tomorrow. (She waits for a reply, but he continues to read the paper.) Dear, are you angry with me?*
>
> *He: No. I'm just tired. (He closes his eyes.)*
>
> *She: Just rest, dear. (Thinks, "Here we go again, the silent treatment." She covers him with a blanket.)*

This entire exchange masks all real feelings. The relationship is dead. Two people living together is not a marriage.

As an exercise, for two weeks, write in your workbook each day the methods you used to avoid potentially unpleasant situations with your partner, children, or friends. Observe your partner and keep a log on his confrontation avoidance techniques. Evaluate these avoidance techniques. Was it worth avoiding?

Sometimes it can be better to skip some unimportant issue if it doesn't leave you with bad feelings. At the end of two weeks, discuss those workbook entries that still make you feel dissatisfied. You can also consider ways to be more direct with each other.

Creative communication is a goal — something we continually strive to reach. You and your partner can practice the skills of creative communication and conflict resolution from this chapter. The skills you develop will be crucial to your progress in your marriage.

Conflict Summary

The purpose of this exercise is to identify specific problem areas in your marriage.

Create in your workbook a list of problem areas in your marriage. Begin by examining an entire week in your life. Look for certain times of the day or certain situations which have caused you anger or frustration. Which of your partner's behaviors are involved? Consider — but don't limit yourself to — the following categories, and list any conflicts that arise in these areas:

1. Sex or money
2. Children, meals, or household problems
3. Communication
4. Vacations, leisure time, free time, schedules
5. Material possessions
6. Friends, careers, other values

From time to time, review the exercises you have done in this chapter and include any conflict areas that were revealed. Pay attention to areas which either of you felt reluctant to discuss or which triggered arguments.

Kinds of Conflict

There are different kinds of conflict: content conflict, value conflict, and ego-conflict. A confrontation based on message accuracy is *content conflict* over a fact, an inference, a definition. These conflicts are the easiest to resolve. Facts can be looked up, inferences can be tested, definitions can be clarified. Even when content conflicts cannot be resolved, they are still easier to cope with because they are more logical than emotional.

The second kind of conflict, which is usually more difficult to resolve, is value conflict. Value conflicts occur when people differ in their views of life, such as religious, political, or social attitudes.

Values cannot be verified and are based primarily on belief systems. We either believe in God or we do not; we believe in social welfare or belief it is destructive; we believe in democracy or think people cannot rule themselves. With a friend, you can enjoy exploring a value difference if you do not intend to change the other person's values.

But in marriage, it is often wiser to acknowledge the difference and allow your partner to believe what he/she wants to believe. These belief differences can be set aside and kept out of your relationship. Save your energy to negotiate such differences as the value of cleanliness, order, money or time.

When we need to win, when our personal image is in danger, *ego conflicts* arise. Judgmental statements about a person's self-concept (intelligent or stupid, graceful or clumsy, pretty or ugly, diligent or lazy) threaten self-esteem and are the most damaging and the most difficult to resolve.

Individuals with a strong sense of self-worth are less vulnerable to attack than those who question their own value. A relationship grows when two people enjoy each other's differences and celebrate each other's uniqueness. We need to learn not only to permit differences but actually rejoice in them.

The Value of Negotiation

Here we begin a discussion of one of the most essential aspects of a good, working marriage — the art of negotiation. By now, if you have read and practiced the previous exercises, your communication process will have improved. However, negotiation refers to the ability to find mutual solutions to problems without either party feeling that he or she has won or lost. The groundwork that forms the foundation for negotiating resolutions to problems includes the following:

1. Define the area of disagreement.
2. Stay in the present (don't dredge up the past).
3. Negotiate *one problem at a time*.
4. Take turns expressing feelings about the problem.
5. Use "I" messages.
6. Without making judgments, brainstorm different solutions.
7. Choose three or four you like.
8. Find one or more you both agree upon.
9. Discuss detailed steps to carry out each solution.
10. After a trial period, reevaluate the solution to see if it is working or if you need to renegotiate a new solution.

Now let's look at the reasons for these steps in negotiating compromises.

Defining the area of disagreement makes clear for each person the issue that causes problems. It provides a foundation for discussing differences without anger. If another unresolved problem comes up, insist upon discussing that issue later. It is important to stay in the present and not divert the discussion to other problems in the past. By focusing on one problem at a time, solutions are

128

more apt to be agreed upon.

The irony of negotiating in a relationship is that the plan itself can become a game for people to get their own way, to win the changes they want, to get others to change their behavior. If true autonomy in the relationship is the goal, each person must be in touch with his or her own motivations and intentions.

In each negotiating process there is an element of compromise, of finding a new solution acceptable to both parties, a solution in which both individuals gain something. Both of you can emerge as winners. The solution does not result from one person manipulating the other or of one using power over the other.

One useful device to apply in measuring how important an issue may be to each partner is to place it on a scale from zero to ten. If to one person the problem and the solution is mildly important, it might be rated a "3". If the other partner feels strongly about the problem and the suggested solution, it might be rated as a "9".

This kind of rating simply allows each person to express the strength or importance of an issue. It communicates levels of importance of any given problem to each person. If used carefully, rating problems and solutions can aid the negotiating process.

After reaching a decision together, the way you follow through with it is most important. If you fall short at the implementation stage, you are back at the beginning.

Later evaluation of the compromise and how it is functioning is also important. If your solution works, the negotiation has been successful. If the solution is not working, you both can go back and work again on the original problem. Don't get locked into your original goals and expectations. Better solutions are always possible. Keep your options open. Successful negotiation includes implementing a workable solution to problems so that both parties gain something in the process.

What Kind of Negotiator Are You?"

There are many styles of negotiating. Observe and rate yourself and your partner by copying the following exercise in your workbook and circling the numbers that you feel are appropriate. Compare your ratings with each other. Do you see yourself as your partner sees you?

Ratings: 1 = Not at all
            2 = A little
            3 = Moderately
            4 = Very

Negotiation style	I am	He (she) is
Manipulative		
Leading		
Following		
Passive		
Threatening		
Peacemaking		
Rational		
Persuasive		

Conflict can result in growth. Some of the positive results are:

To find the truth about yourself
To share different perceptions of the world
To find out the truth about your partner
To find your distortions or self-deceptions
To share different views of reality with a loved one

In every relationship, some differences may be irreconcilable. To avoid endless dispute when a conflict becomes unresolvable, say,

"I feel we cannot resolve this issue. I want to let it go at at this time. We can disagree without jeopardizing our relationship. I do not want to merge my identity with yours on this issue. I want some separate views of my own. We share a great deal that is positive. I love you very much, and I want to let this issue go at this time."

Re-negotiate

In a marriage, problems come up daily because of differences in perception, interests, needs, goals, and personalities. Through constructive processes such as conflict resolution and negotiation, many, although not all, of your marital disagreements can be resolved to some degree of satisfaction. However, it would be a mistake to rigidly enforce any agreement.

Agreements are compromises that fit a particular moment in time. Once some agreement has been reached where some degree of mutual give and take is put into practice, the results must be reevaluated. Only a child says, "You promised! You promised!" Adults know that agreements are open to change just as contracts are negotiated and renegotiated.

All contracts, agreements, commitments are open to renegotiation. In addition to motivating growth, education, and improving living conditions, conflict provides a source of stimulation. If all your needs were met, you would create new ones. If you had no conflicts, you would create some.

In your marriage, you can learn to manage conflict constructively through accurate communication, trust, negotiations, cooperative resolutions, and caring for the well-being of both the self and the spouse.

10 The Marital Checkup

There is considerable doubt. . .marriage counseling is effective at all compared to the individual's efforts in his or her own behalf.

Gerhard Neubeck

For medical and dental health, an annual visit to a doctor and a dentist are routine for most people who value their health. The procedures are familiar. You make appointments, go to the doctor's and dentist's office, check-in at a desk, and allow the doctor and dentist to examine you.

The doctor asks questions. "Have there been any changes in your health recently? Any pain or discomfort? How are you eating and sleeping?" You answer these questions about how your body is functioning. Finally, lab tests such as x-rays, blood and urine samples are taken to reveal conditions not visible to the eye.

Benefits like those from medical and dental examinations can result from regular marital checkups. You can conduct your own marital examination by using this chapter as a guide. Every couple can benefit. Your purpose is similar to the medical examination. In most cases your doctor says, "Your health is good." The marital checkup tells you if your marriage is excellent, good, or fair. It can uncover marital problems before they threaten your marriage. You can use preventive measures before they reach a crisis that requires professional attention.

When you conduct a checkup simply to verify that your marital health is good, this technique can enrich your relationship and help you set goals for future growth.

Notice how you and your spouse react to the idea of conduct-

133

ing your own marital examination. The following are common questions asked or statements made about a marital checkup:

1. *Why do we need a checkup for our marriage?*
    The checkup is a positive, preventive process that can help every couple assess where they are today and where they want to be tomorrow. You can identify small problems and treat them before they mushroom into crises that threaten your marriage. You can also use the checkup as a catalyst for the growth and enrichment of a relationship that is already healthy.

2. *I am happy with the way things are now.*
    No relationship remains static. Relationships change. If you feel satisfied with your marriage, use this checkup as a guarantee of continued happiness. Identify the things in your relationship that are successful and build them into future plans. But more importantly, the checkup is a way to find out if your partner is also content with your marriage.

3. *If we probe into our marriage, it might start trouble.*
    What will happen if you don't probe? Will potential problems go away if they are hidden or ignored? Facing reality is far better than hiding behind fear. Intimacy can be the reward for in-depth communication with your spouse.
    In grading a student, a teacher gives an A, B, or C grade. Even an A grade can be improved with more information. You may find your marriage is in the "A" category which can verify what both of you feel about your marriage. On the other hand, if some small problem gets buried, it can, like a volcano, erupt out of proportion in a totally inappropriate way. Marital difficulties, like diseases, are readily treatable in early stages but can be fatal when they go undetected.

4. *I am afraid to check up on my relationship.*
    Similarly, many people are afraid to go to the doctor and the dentist. Like an ostrich with his head stuck in the sand, they prefer living with fear to having a doctor verify a problem they suspect. Fear of examining a relationship can result from an unwillingness to disagree, to communicate,

134

or to admit that unresolved problems exist.

The real fear, however, is that the marriage will end in divorce. You can learn ways to overcome your fears. It's possible the problem you fear in the relationship exists more in your imagination than in reality.

Most experts agree that marital relationships go through cycles and phases. Life stages are natural and can best be handled by shifts or changes in the nature of your interaction with your partner. Self-examination of your marriage, therefore, is a way to recognize the natural evolution of life, to anticipate changes, to prevent problems, or to resolve conflicts.

Take Stock of Your Marriage

The remainder of this chapter consists of exercises to help you do your own marriage checkup. Before you begin, here are some suggestions to help assure you that the process will work and even be enjoyable.

1. Hopefully, both you and your partner will be willing to complete the exercises. Take a light approach. This can be a fun game to bring you closer — something you can do together. However, if your spouse is strongly unwilling to spend time playing with this checkup, *don't insist.* Your marriage will benefit if just one of you becomes more aware of its dynamics. One-sided intimacy is an improvement over no intimacy at all.

2. Assuming your spouse is willing to play, reread the introduction to this chapter together. Set up an appointment when you both agree to work on the exercises. Choose a time when neither of you will feel pressured or preoccupied with other matters.

3. Schedule your checkup time for at least forty-five minutes but feel free to work longer if you are comfortable continuing.

4. Be flexible. If you begin an exercise and you are tired or can't concentrate, reschedule your meeting for a later time. (If this happens often, it may be a sign that one or both of you wants to avoid the process.)

5. It is important, especially if you and your spouse are uneasy about embarking upon a close look at your marriage, to be relaxed when you begin. Here is an exercise to help

you relax:

First tighten all your muscles, then relax them to loosen up muscle tension. Flex the muscles in your hands and feet several times. Check to see if your muscles are tight across your shoulders or at the base of your skull or in your neck. Check to see if your face muscles and the muscles around your mouth and eyes are relaxed. Notice any tension in your body and relax that tension.

Now that your body muscles are relaxed, sit together in a comfortable position. Hold hands. Close your eyes and visualize a beautiful scene — a beach, a lake, or snow-clad mountains — preferably a place you and your partner have enjoyed together.

Breathe deeply several times. Each time, as you exhale, say to yourself, "Relax." Let your muscles fall loose — your arms, shoulders, torso, and legs. Imagine yourself completely relaxed. Then concentrate upon the stillness within yourself.

Take ten or fifteen minutes to relax. Then open your eyes. Most people who practice relaxation can relax in a few minutes. After a period of relaxation, most people feel alert and revitalized.

In your workbook, make a page for each of the following exercises. Answer as authentically as you can. There are no right or wrong answers. You *always* have the right to "pass" on any question that feels too threatening. Then, at a later date, you can go back to unanswered questions, if you wish.

*   *   *   *

Self-Disclosure Questionnaire

This questionnaire contains a number of items about different aspects of self-disclosure. First, read the statement. Then in your workbook, fill in the appropriate response from the 1 (least) to 5 (most) scale. Ask yourself for each question, "How free do I feel in disclosing myself to my partner?"

Each of these questions, of course, could become a topic of dialogue with your partner, but the function at this point is simply to reveal yourself to yourself. Read the following statements and ask yourself how important (5) or how unimportant (1) is it for you to disclose the following issues to your partner.

Unimportant				Important
1	2	3	4	5

1. Aspects of my personality that I like/dislike
2. Feelings toward my spouse that I like/dislike
3. Things in my past or present that I feel good/ashamed of or guilty about
4. Things I feel angry about
5. Things I feel depressed about
6. Things I feel anxious about or afraid of
7. Things I feel hurt about
8. Things I feel proud and elated about
9. How I wish I looked – my image of the ideal appearance
10. Whether ornot I have any health problems (trouble sleeping, digestion, allergies, headaches, etc.)
11. Whether or not I have any long-range worries or concerns about my health (cancer, ulcers, heart conditions)
12. My feelings about our sexual relationship
13. Problems I have had with my parents and siblings
14. Feelings I now have about my parents and siblings
15. Concerns I have had about my parent's relationship
16. Concerns about my role in my relationship with other family members
17. What I like most/least about my partner as a companion
18. What I like most about my partner as a lover
19. What I feel uncomfortable about with my partner as a lover
20. What I like most/least about my partner as a parent
21. What I like most/least about the way my partner joins in family fun
22. What I appreciate most about the way my partner shares family responsibilities
23. What I want most from my partner that I feel I am not getting.

After completing this questionnaire, before sharing anything with your partner, ask yourself what you learned new about yourself? Were you surprised by the number of areas that you do not discuss with your partner?

*   *   *   *

Many people are amazed to discover how many intimate

thoughts, desires, and angers they have locked away in little mental cages hidden from their partner.

Madge, for example, had been married for eleven years when she came for counseling. After filling out the self-disclosure questionnaire, she said,

> *It's uncanny. I felt like someone was groping around touching all my nerve endings. Some of the questions touched where I spend a lot of time being angry but trying not to show it. Others were like deep bruises I never knew were there. I wondered, anxiously, how my husband would respond if I really opened up. I also wondered what he might write about the same questions.*

Sharing Self-Disclosure Results

In going over this questionnaire, find some issues that you might feel comfortable sharing with your husband or wife. At first, it is easier to share positive feelings than negative ones.

Before sharing this information, agree with your spouse not to ask "Why?" or answer with "Because?" *Why-because* leads to rationalizations and justifications or self-deception. It's enough to simply share information. It is appropriate to ask, "Can you give me an example?" or "When does (or did) this feeling occur?"

Examine your resistance to self-disclosure. None, all, or some of the following may apply. Resistance is usually complex.

> Is it that you simply do not know yourself very well?
> Is it that you don't trust your partner?
> Has your partner ever used shared information against you?
> Do you think of yourself as a "private" person who does not relate on an intimate level?
> Is it that you've simply acquired a habit of *not* sharing information or being intimate with your mate?

Write down, in your notebook, your thoughts about your resistance to revealing yourself. Include your anxieties and fears. Whatever your reasons, if sharing and being close is one of your goals, give yourself time to build greater mutual trust. Tell your partner that you are sharing information you do not want shared with any other person.

Disclosing the self involves being vulnerable. Begin with the safest items and move toward revealing more sensitive information so that you will gradually build a higher level of trust.

Self-disclosure, like most qualities, lies on a continuum from a little trust to more trust. We cannot demand that anyone disclose themselves. Although there will always be certain areas that each of us wants to keep secret, trusting can be satisfying, rewarding, and exciting as you learn to relate more intimately.

Do You Really Like Yourself?

Following is another questionnaire designed to reveal how well you like yourself. Sometimes you may treat your partner, co-work-, ers, relatives, or children poorly because you do not feel good about yourself. It's as if you need an external target for inner hostilities. Many of us use those closest to us when we are angry about our own mistakes or faults and release angry feelings upon others.

Self-Esteem Questionnaire

When you feel good about yourself, you are more apt to treat others in a civil manner. On this questionnaire, the first step is to identify problems. The next step is to try to find solutions. Answer the questions as honestly as you can. Enter the number in your notebook which best describes how well you like yourself.

1	2	3	4	5
Never	Rarely	Seldom	Occasionally	Always

1. If someone hurts my feelings, I tell them so.
2. People value my opinions.
3. I feel intelligent.
4. Nothing is too good for me.
5. There's not much about me that I'd really like to change.
6. I rarely compare myself with other people to see if I rate higher or lower than they.
7. I enjoy meeting and talking with new people.
8. I feel comfortable at parties.
9. There aren't many people I would change places with.
10. I'm glad to be who I am.
11. If I had my life to live over, I wouldn't change much.
12. I like the place where I live.

13. I enjoy my work.
14. People generally admire me.
15. I'm a kind person.
16. I like to get up in the morning.
17. I can take care of myself.
18. Other people need me.
19. I watch what I eat, get proper exercise, and take good care of myself.
20. I lead a balanced life: sleep, work, and play.
21. I enjoy being by myself.
22. Most of the time, I am satisfied with my life.
23. I see myself as an attractive person.
24. I see myself as a loving person.
25. I see myself as a sharing person.

Add up the number of points. A score of 125, which is 100%, would be unrealistic. Rarely are any of us so invulnerable as to rate that kind of score. However, the higher your total score, the higher your self-esteem.

If you find your score is not as high as you would wish, choose from these 25 statement areas that you would like to improve.

*   *   *   *

If you find you often don't feel good about yourself, you have a lot of company. We live in a negative time and culture. It seems easier and more common for people to criticize themselves and others than it is to give positive, loving comments. Few of us ever feel so positive about ourselves that we become invulnerable to criticism. And, in most cases, we are our own worst critics.

You can do certain things to start feeling better about yourself. You can begin each day by looking in the mirror and saying, "Good morning. Today is going to be a good day."

We actually have the power to make each day a wonderful day. We can give ourselves honest credit for the good things we do. Few of us give ourselves credit for the things we do well, yet we are sharply critical of our mistakes.

We have a tremendous power with the use of language. Instead of thinking in terms of "right" and "wrong," you can say, "That worked." Or "That didn't work. . .so now I'll try something else."

Very few of our decisions are irreversible. When we make a decision and put it into action, that action either works or does not work. If it does *not* work, we can try something else until we find what works or solves a particular situation.

It is axiomatic that you cannot love others unless you first love yourself. Caring for the self leads to a better life. In *The Virtue of Selfishness*, Ayn Rand says that unless you take care of your own needs, you will not be good for those around you. The wife who plays martyr to please others or the husband who denies his own needs to impress others usually ends up resenting the very persons for whom they denied themselves.

An example of low self-esteem is Leonard who in any situation of conflict with his wife blames himself. In trying to work against this tendency, Leonard discovered that he was judging himself according to the very harsh judgments his father had used against him as a child. Leonard said:

> *Dad used to whip me whenever I did something wrong. He called me a lousy brat. It didn't matter if it was a little thing or not. He always jumped on me. I felt that I could not do anything right.*

Leonard discovered that he was transferring these "father" messages into his marriage. He blamed himself for everything. Finally Leonard learned to play a game with himself. When something went wrong, he pretended to be another person talking to himself. He would say, "Alright, I didn't like what you did just then. But I like *you* even if I don't like what you did."

When we can separate a deed from the person, we can make changes in our behavior. Inside each of us is a person who can change those behaviors we do not like at the same time we can like the person we are.

Another technique for a person with low self-esteem is to write in their notebook three things they like about themselves. This list of positive qualities can be added to each day.

Another positive reinforcement is to carry on a dialogue with yourself. "I like the way I handled that situation." And "I feel good about that job I completed today." Begin to "pat yourself on the back." Write down even small accomplishments in your notebook, and turn to them when you are feeling bad about yourself.

Most of us do not have to worry about inflated egos. We can benefit by giving ourselves credit for those things we do well rather than criticizing ourselves for everything. This approval may carry over to others so that we begin to give positive feedback to those people we live and work with. We can develop the habit of thinking positively about ourselves and others.

Disagreement

Now that you've taken an honest assessment of yourself, the next thing to realize is that *no close relationship can exist with another person without some disagreements*. If we are open in expressing our opinions and feelings, we are willing to agree and disagree *equally*, to express both positive and negative feelings as equals.

Most of us have been around a person who does nothing but tell us "nice things" about ourselves. Soon their comments become meaningless. Similarly, the person who does nothing but criticize is a person we want to avoid. The individual who balances both the positive and negative comments becomes a valuable friend because his or her comments have meaning.

The following questionnaire tests your depth of feelings for agreeing or disagreeing with your partner. Again, there are no right or wrong answers; yet the answers can give you a better idea of how you see things and what you feel in your relationship with your partner.

Once you have completed answering questions by yourself, share answers with your partner. This sharing can become a measure of the depth and completeness of your communication with each other. You will not see yourself or your *interaction* in exactly the same way as you did before your explorations.

The Dyadic Adjustment Scale

The dyadic adjustment scale is a scale that includes the most important issues in the life of a married couple. There are fifteen issues mentioned. Feel free to add any points which uniquely fit your marriage. Dyadic means "two". Adjustment implies the ability to find creative solutions to differences so that both partners in the marriage are satisfied.

In your notebook, answer each question as accurately as possible.

5	4	3	2	1	0
Always Agree	Almost Always Agree	Occa- sionally Disagree	Fre- quently Disagree	Almost Always Disagree	Always Disagree

1. Handing family finances
2. Matters of recreation
3. Religious matters

4. Demonstrations of affection
5. Friends
6. Sex
7. Conventionality (correct/proper behavior)
8. Philosophy of life
9. Ways of dealing with parents or in-laws
10. Goals (give examples)
11. Amount of time spent together
12. Making major decisions
13. Household tasks
14. Leisure time interests and activities
15. Career decisions

*   *   *   *

In sharing the results of The Dyadic Adjustment Scale with your partner, you will find differences. What is important is to look at those differences and discuss how you feel about them. You can appreciate your differences and enjoy your individuality.

Marital Appraisal

The purpose of this exercise is to assess your current satisfaction in marriage. Each partner writes his and her answers separately. Write as authentically as you can. You need not share any particular answer if you are not ready to share. You can simply say, "I want to work on this issue by myself for a while. Perhaps it is my problem."

No set of questions could be written that fits every individual because of uniqueness in human beings. Nor can any set of questions be written that fits every relationship. Therefore, feel free to reword the following questions in a way that makes them more applicable to you personally and to your marriage. If any question reminds you of other questions, write those questions down for a later discussion after you have completed those listed here.

A. Draw a line down the center of your paper dividing it into two halves. In the first column, list elements you *like* in your marriage — the things that work well for you. (For example, a beautiful home, a good salary, he/she is handsome/beautiful; intelligent/kind; thoughtful/fun, etc.)

In the second column, list those elements you *dislike* in your marriage, things you have difficulty accepting. (For example:

He/she is stingy/thoughtless; we bicker too much; we don't have enough time together, etc.)

B. On a second page of your notebook, answer the following:
    1. Do you look forward to being with your partner after being separated during the day?
(If you answer "NO", write down the major reason why you dread going home.
If you answer "YES", write down what you look forward to as you go home.)
    2. What does the word "Love" mean to you? Share your definition with your partner.
    3. Does the word love mean that the security and well-being of your partner is as important to you as your own security and well-being?
    4. Do you feel that your spouse loves you, no matter how you've defined love?
    5. List what you feel are five instances of your own loving behavior toward your partner in the last month.
    6. List what you feel are five instances of your partner's loving behavior toward you in the past month.
    7. List five unloving things you have done — intentionally or unintentionally — in the past month.
    8. List five unloving things your partner has done in the past month.
    9. List five things you have asked your partner to do which he or she has not done.
    10. List five things your partner has asked you to do which you have not done.
    11. List five things you wish your partner could change about him or herself.
    12. Review questions 9, 10, and 11. List reasons why you think both you and your partner are unwilling to do things or to make changes.

C. Discussion: Compare your answers from Parts A and B. Conclude your discussion by answering *together* the following two questions:
    1. Do I believe our marriage is so good that there is little we can do to make it better? (If either person answers "no", answer number 2.)
    2. Do we want to explore ways that might improve our relationship? If the answer is "yes", go onto the next exercise.

Interpersonal Comparison Tests

The purpose of this exercise is to assess individual feelings about self, marriage, and life. With some questions, more than one answer may fit. If no answer fits your situation, write a sentence describing that issue in your marriage.

*   *   *   *

Complete each statement below by selecting the answer that comes closest to your feelings *today*. Be sure that both of you answer *all* of the questions. Do the exercise separately. Do not compare notes until you both have finished.

Present Life Experiences
1. Financially and socially, I feel the next five years
    a. will be reasonably successful.
    b. will consist of two steps forward and one back.
    c. are impossible to predict at present.
    d. scare me.

2. About my health, I would say that
    a. I have always had and expect to have perfect health.
    b. For the last few years, my general health has been below par, but I believe I'll regain excellent health soon.
    c. I don't know. I guess I'm healthy, but I haven't had a physical for years.
    d. I often feel tired and without energy.

3. About my emotional adjustment, I would say that
    a. I feel fairly secure emotionally.
    b. I am happiest when I live with someone
    c. I do not think about my emotions.

4. With regard to children
    a. I don't feel that I am (or would be) a good parent.
    b. I know that I am (or would be) a good parent.
    c. I think my marriage would be most successful *without* children
    d. I would like to have _____ children.

5. With regard to being married at this particular time, I feel
    a. I am glad I am married.
    b. I married to please my friends and relatives.

145

c.   I have some doubts about whether I should be married.

The Person I Am Married To

1.   My partner's appearance
     a.   is extremely attractive
     b.   is satisfactory
     c.   means little because I look for qualities other than physi-cal attractiveness
     d.   embarrasses me.

2.   My partner's family
     a.   my partner comes from a family I admire.
     b.   my partner comes from a family I feel a part of.
     c.   I have little connection with his/her family.
     d.   I find my partner's family irritating.

3.   Regarding similarities between the parents and my partner
     a.   I worry that she/he may become too much like his/her mother/father.
     b.   I do not feel his/her parents play any significant role in our marriage.
     c.   I do not think he/she is like either of his/her parents.

4.   With regard to marriage, my partner and I
     a.   have discussed our doubts about our marriage.
     b.   have doubts we do not discuss.
     c.   are afraid of hurting each other by discussing our prob-lems.
     d.   do not have any doubts or fears whatsoever.

5.   With regard to *our* marriage,
     a.   at times, I wish to end the marriage.
     b.   although I have doubts, I wish to stay in it.
     c.   I feel that I can overcome any doubts since my love is great enough.
     d.   I would have doubts no matter whom I had married. I do not let these doubts spoil my marriage.

Marriage and Profession

1.   With regard to my occupational/avocational interests,
     a.   I do not believe my marriage and my interests conflict.
     b.   I feel that I would sacrifice almost anything for a happy marriage.

c. I believe I can pursue both my marriage and my interests even when they conflict.

d. My partner has no professional commitments that would jeopardize or interfere with our marriage.

e. My partner's commitment to his/her career is something I admire and support.

f. my partner's commitment to his/her career could jeopardize our marriage.

2. With regard to the future of our marriage,
   a. I worry about financial problems.
   b. I worry about in-law problems.
   c. I'm troubled about having children.
   d. I worry that my partner might have an affair.
   e. I don't worry about things until they happen.

3. With regard to companionship, my spouse and I
   a. have many interests in common.
   b. have independent interests and are supportive of each other's activities.
   c. expect to develop interests in common.
   d. seem to have little in common when we are not busy with social activities.

Discussion

After both of you have completed the questions, share your answers. Note those answers that agree. Ask questions about those answers that differ. Ask each other the following:

1. How can we utilize our "sameness" to increase the solidarity of our marriage?
2. How can we neutralize our differences or turn them into advantages?

Listening

The purpose of this exercise is to determine how *accurately* you listen to each other. Limit each person to ten or fifteen minutes for each step of the discussion. Do not attribute anything to your partner except what is actually said.

1. One person begins by making statements that begin with "The characteristics I would like to see in you to make

147

our marriage more positive for me are. . ."

2. The second person summarizes the comments made by the first. "I hear you as saying you wish that I. . ." Simply restate what your partner has said without adding information, defending, or giving reasons.

3. Reverse roles. The partner who spoke first now listens, and as listener takes a turn at summarizing.

4. Repeat the same process with the words, "It sounds as if I could improve the situation if I. . . ."

5. Repeat the same process using the words, "I would be willing to improve this situation by. . ."

Follow-Up Discussion

Give yourself a day or two to think of ways in which you could do something that would improve your marriage. In this follow-up discussion, list three things you would be willing to do. For example:

1. I would be willing to call you whenever I am going to be late.

2. I will spend Saturday afternoons with the children while you have free time.

Communication

One of the purposes of these exercises is to help you understand the status of communication in your relationship. Review the chapter on communication. For now, simply answer each question "yes" or "no"; then explain what you mean and describe the situation giving specific examples.

This exercise may be done either by talking or by writing in your workbook. However, if you write it out, you will have more time to recall specific examples.

1. Do you feel satisfied with your communication with your partner most of the time? (Give an example)

2. Is your partner a good listener?

3. Does your partner listen to both the content and the *feeling* of your communication?

4. Do you have difficulty communicating your feelings, thoughts, on any particular subjects?

5. Are you often frustrated when you try to communicate?

6. When do you feel good about your communication?

148

The marital checkup can help identify specific areas which need attention. In these exercises, you will continue to uncover some areas you would like to improve in your relationship.

Make sure that you and your partner both agree that a certain action needs to be taken. It is important to find out if *both* of you are willing to work on problems. If you have not done so before, affirm this point with your partner *now*. Share your thoughts and feelings about what you want changed. Listen as your partner tells what he/she wants. Determine if you both are willing to learn the skills necessary to make changes.

Your marriage is changing all the time whether you direct those changes or not. At the same time, each of you is constantly in transition in your individual life. Much of the time, you are not aware of these changes. We all have a tendency to treat each other the way we were in the past rather than the way we are in the present. We must constantly remind ourselves that we are changing and our marriage is changing. Repeating this marital checkup at different stages of your marriage can help you explore the transitions in your relationship so that you can both move together to the next stage.

11 The Art of Negotiating the Marriage Contract

As we've seen throughout this book, the most important skill two individuals can use to make a relationship successful is the art of negotiating.

The word "contract" may seem to be a cold and rigid way to express the physical, mental, and emotional closeness of a marital relationship. Yet, we live each day of our lives responding to written or unwritten contracts, either abiding by them or violating them.

Each time you stop your car at a stoplight you fulfill a contract to protect your safety and that of others. Each morning when you get out of bed and get to work on time, you are fulfilling a contract with your employer and more importantly, with your partner to whom you have committed an expenditure of time and energy to insure your financial security together. Whenever you cook breakfast or mow the lawn, you are fulfilling a piece of the contract with your partner.

A contract, therefore, is nothing more than a clear presentation of the commitments two people make to each other. If you and your partner have worked together through the preceding chapters of this book, you have already gained awareness and sensitivity to problem areas in your relationship. We've seen how in many, if not all, cases being able to compromise is an important way to avoid crisis. But in order to compromise, you both must have a clear understanding of what the "rules" of your relationship are, what's important to both of you, and where you can and cannot compromise. It is for this reason — even though you may have been living according to unwritten rules between you — that we recommend that you write a specific contract governing your relationship and then renew and rewrite it at regular intervals.

Marriage Vows

Isn't love enough? Aren't our marriage vows enough?

The answer is *no*. Love is not enough to account for individual differences and needs. Marriage vows are not enough because even though they may be "binding" in a civil or religious sense, the marriage ritual was designed to cover general situations and again does not consider individual differences and needs.

Consider for a moment what we pledge to do during the marriage ceremony. We vow "to have and to hold, to cherish, and, in some cases, obey, for better or for worse." These are beautiful and valid vows, but what do they mean in terms of day-to-day living? What does it mean for you, two individuals, to have and to hold? How firmly do you hold? Who obeys whom? Does for better or for worse mean that you must cling to each other no matter how bad your relationship may become?

Unfortunately, many of the answers to these questions are not clear until couples reach the divorce courts. There's no telling how many relationships might have been saved by realistic marriage contracts, but I do know that I've used the approach successfully with hundreds of couples. For a number of years, I have guided couples, who had been married from one year to thirty, in writing marriage contracts. Many of these faced a crisis that had only two solutions: dissolving their marriage, or trying to straighten out their problems and establishing healthier patterns.

These individuals were not looking for prolonged, in-depth counseling. They were hurting and needed a direct approach — guidance in dealing with their *present* hurts. They needed to evaluate their relationships and arrive at marriage contracts which accounted for, and provided for, their *separate* needs and their *combined* needs. A new marriage contract, as many of them found, can mark the rebirth of a relationship.

Other couples see the marriage contract as a tool for enhancing an already healthy and happy marriage. Thus, marriage enrichment is another goal for writing such a contract. Marriages need renewal and enrichment just as soil needs organic material added each season to insure a healthier bloom.

Ideally, a detailed marriage contract should be written and then reviewed under the following conditions:

1. *Before* marriage.
2. Periodically — perhaps once a year — after marriage, to determine if the contract is fulfilling the needs and desires of both partners. Make it part of your anniversary cele-

bration.

3.   Whenever problems arise and before crises occur.

An important fact to remember is that *it is never too late in a marriage to write a contract for enrichment or problem-solving*.

How Do We Start?

Divide all the items in your marriage contract into two groups:

Essentials and Negotiables

Divide the essentials into feelings, wants, needs, commitments, values, etc., and do the same with the negotiables.

Let us suppose you are contemplating marriage. What do you and your proposed partner need to know about yourselves as individuals, and about each other, in order to create a sound and comprehensive contract?

First, you must examine yourself — knowing and defining one's dreams, expectations, ambitions, emotions, strengths and weaknesses, one's mind, body, and feelings, is necessary. Remember, a contract is a commitment. It is an agreement between two people to do something to and for each other. To do this, each must know what his or her own needs are. In a marriage, the partners choose to live together and share their lives because this seems to offer the greatest rewards for them. What makes it rewarding is the balance of freedom, the commitment they accept, and the personal needs which they fulfill for their partner and themselves.

As a first step, compare your life alone with the life you anticipate with your partner. Or, if you are already living in an intimate relationship, recall those areas which you found satisfying while living alone along with those in which you needed to share with someone else for fulfillment.

Use your workbook and ask yourself, "When I was living alone, what were my ten most important needs?"

List anything that comes to mind. Write your answers spontaneously. List more than ten if you can. Here are some examples:

A neat apartment
Books and records
Personal freedom
Friends
Nice clothes

A satisfying job
Financial independence
A constant companion
A lover
Physical comfort
Parties
Attending sports events
Participating in sports
Attending the theater
Vacationing in the snow
A balanced diet
Regular exercise
Soaking in a hot tub
Talking on the phone
Playing cards and games

Remember, this is your personal list. It helps to identify you to your partner. Some of the above items may fit you, while others do not. Once you have completed this list, rearrange the items in order of importance to you and compare them with your partner's list.

Once you have completed this part of the exercise, answer the question, "What are the ten most important things I want from an intimate relationship or marriage?"

Love
Companionship
Understanding
Support
Caring and comfort
Friendship
Intellectual challenge
Emotional closeness
Physical closeness
Sex
Sharing a home
Having children
Trust
Commitment
Travel together
Escape from loneliness
Partner as adviser
Partner as confidante

Again, do not be confined to these. When you are finished, list the top ten needs and desires in order of importance. This list may include some items from your first list but note, of course, that there are certain things you can have with a partner but not when you are alone. Also, you may note that the opposite is true — that marriage may limit the satisfaction of some needs and freedoms that you've enjoyed as a single person. In comparing the second list with the first list, you and your partner will learn what is most important to each of you, and begin to measure — realistically — what you are capable of providing for each other. If you are already married, this comparison may reveal areas of need which you are *not* satisfying for your partner, or vice versa. It may also be the first time you are aware of certain wishes and desires. As we have said repeatedly, your partner may not be aware of your needs unless you express them, and you can't ask if you don't know your own needs.

Throughout this preliminary examination, which will lead to your marriage contract, you are teaching yourself to think in specific terms rather than vague generalities so that you learn what you may expect of each other. Again using your workbook, you can refine the process further by asking yourself the following questions.

1. What will make me happy? Is it money or possessions? Is it undying love and devotion? Is it children? Is it security? Or is it a combination of these with other things? Answer as explicitly as you can.

2. What are my dreams and fantasies? Do I imagine my husband to be a masterful lover who carries me away to a life of ease and luxury, or do I dream of an ordinary man with whom to share whatever life has to offer? Do I dream of a gorgeous but virtuous wife envied by all the men around me, or a woman who will walk with me steadfastly through triumphs and failures? What is *your* dream?

3. What do I want to have in a year, five years, ten years, twenty years, from now? For most of us, it is a big order to set goals this far in the future, but you will deepen and broaden your understanding of each other by setting down your thoughts on this. Do you want to own a home, have healthy children? Do you want to be a successful doctor or lawyer? Do you want to be a highly successful career woman with children, without children, before or after having children? Each of you may spend an entire evening answering this question.

155

4. What are my ambitions as an individual? To be a great surgeon? An operatic soprano? President of a corporation or home decorating agency? . . .as part of a couple? To be a good father or mother? Sharing in the care of our home and family?
    For us as a couple? To be comfortably wealthy? To enjoy travel and many friends? To be widely respected in our community?
5. What are my strengths and what are my weaknesses?
6. What are my partner's strengths and weaknesses?

These last two are difficult questions to answer and we have not suggested answers because this is a very personal matter between you and your partner. Needless to say, it is necessary to answer both questions fully and honestly if you are to come to a realistic marriage contract. Once you've answered these questions, you'll be able to see clearly where the two of you may not be seeing eye-to-eye and where you are.

The final step in your individual examinations is to answer the following questions.

1. Who are we as a unit?
2. What are our strengths and weaknesses as a couple?
3. What are our individual needs?

After you've answered these questions separately, compare your answers. How are they similar and different? Where differences exist, do you see ways in which you can compromise?

This is the heart of your marriage contract — full clarification of your needs and full understanding of what you can and cannot fulfill for your partner. For example, if he asks for your lifelong promise of fidelity and emotional security, can you honestly commit yourself in writing to provide these to him or her? If not, what are the limitations on your commitment. Can you promise these things for a year? If so, write it that way in the contract, with an option to renew that promise or renegotiate it at the end of the year. If he is unsure that he can provide one of your deepest needs — financial security — perhaps you can negotiate this point. Perhaps the contract clause will say that you promise to work *together* toward financial security.

In this fashion, work down through your lists of essential needs, and write each of your small agreements into the larger one.

At this point, you are probably emotionally exhausted, but

you will have cleared away much of the ambiguity and false romantic pictures you may have made of your love and marriage. Your steps toward negotiations for a contract should be a fair and realistic representation of what you — as two individuals — can do for each other in your intimate relationship.

Now, also, it is perhaps safe to tell you that you've covered the most difficult part. You've dealt with the deepest emotional needs. Now you can move onto a series of mini- or sub-contracts dealing with the day-to-day issues of life. Write agreements to cover at least the following:

1. Money
2. Household management
3. Children
4. Friends and social activities
5. Recreation and vacations
6. Professional life

Money

Here are some points to cover on the question of money.

1. Will one person or both be responsible for earning?
2. Will one person control how the money is spent, or will this be handled by joint agreement?
3. Does one of you want to be responsible for bill-paying and handling the checkbook, or will you take turns handling this monthly chore?
4. Will you combine your incomes, or keep separate accounts?
5. Will one or both of you handle budgeting problems?
6. Will one of you receive a weekly or monthly allowance from the paycheck or will you decide upon expenditures jointly? Will each of you have freedom to spend minor amounts of money without accounting to the other? What limits will you set?

Resolve your money issues into a mini-contract before moving on to the next issue. It doesn't matter in what form your contract is written. Use your own language, your own words. Just begin by saying that you two agree to the following, and make sure you both sign all contracts and their renewals and even have witnesses if you feel it will help "legitimize" the contract for you both.

157

Household Management

There are really two parts to this mini-contract: (1) your place and style of living, and (2) responsibility for household management and work. Following are some questions to help you get started.

1. If you had a free choice, where would you want to live? A cabin in the hills? A house in the suburbs? An apartment in the city?
2. In the home of your choice, does each of you need separate rooms to insure private space for those times when you need to be apart?
3. Do you want a small, cozy dwelling or a large, ostentatious house with expensive furniture?
4. Do you want to care for a large lawn with trees and flowers or are these things unimportant to you?
5. When it comes to household work, will you cling to the traditional male-female roles in which the woman does all the cooking and housework, or will you share these duties?
6. Will you take turns washing dishes and laundry?
7. Will you take turns cleaning house, or find a division of duties acceptable to both of you? (For example, perhaps the husband does not mind cleaning bathrooms while his wife prefers to do the vacuuming.)
8. Will one or both of you be responsible for yardwork?
9. Will one or both of you be responsible for automobile maintenance?

Children

Again, this is a two-part contract: (1) Will we have children, and (2) if so, how will we share childcare duties?

The contract must deal with the professional ambitions of both partners, particularly the woman's because she is the one who must cope with pregnancy.

You may decide that you want many children, or none.

If you want children, without interrupting the wife's study or professional career, you may decide to adopt.

If both of you are sure you want at least one child but are uncertain of your parental capabilities to handle more than that, you may agree to have one baby (assuming, of course, that this is possible), and then renegotiate the contract after that baby is born.

Once you come to agreement on having children, the next step is to negotiate a contract detailing the duties of childcare. Some

158

questions to consider are:

1. Will mother be entirely responsible for childcare, diaper washing, and training until the child reaches preschool age, or will father share in these duties?
2. Will one parent be the disciplinarian or will both share this duty?
3. Who will get up in the night for feedings or to comfort a child who is ill? Will you alternate?

You may have every good intention of sharing fully in these matters, but it is important to write down as many details as possible in your contract *before* you embark upon parenthood.

Friends and Social Activities

Referring again to previous chapters, carefully consider your needs and wishes in this realm, and then write down your agreements and compromises.

1. Will you agree to accept each other's friends freely and completely?
2. Will you give each other freedom to spend some time alone with your particular friends?
3. Will you be jealous of opposite-sex friendships?
4. How far are you willing to trust your partner in opposite-sex friendships?
5. What types of recreation do each of you prefer? Sports? Theater? Dinner parties? Drinking and dancing?
6. Can you agree to share all of these with each other, or enjoy some of them alone or with other friends?
7. Will you take an extended vacation every year, or break up your vacations into smaller segments, such as weekends?
8. Where do you prefer to vacation? The beach? Camping? The mountains? Visiting historic sites? If your tastes differ, your contract should contain an agreement as to how you will divide up these activities.
9. Do you enjoy quiet and relaxation when you go away, or the social whirl and excitement of resort centers? Again, find a balance between your wishes.

Professional Life

A most vital mini-contract, as part of your overall marriage contract, is that dealing with your professional ambitions and those of your partner.

1. If your husband has political ambitions, can you enjoy moving in his shadow and even helping him to attain office? If you can, or cannot, say so clearly.
2. Do you object to your wife working outside the home?
3. Do you object to her studying for advanced professional degrees and subsequent practice?
4. Can you give each other complete freedom to follow your own professional aspirations?

These questions should be clearly and pragmatically answered in the premarital contract, and then renegotiated periodically if and when conflicts arise.

Go through all of the areas we've focused on in this book, and cover them in mini-contracts. You can negotiate about your families, about communication (How much is enough? Should we set aside time? etc.), about time, intimacy, in fact, any aspect of your marriage that you both feel should be spelled out and defined in this manner.

12 Marriage Enrichment

*What we need most is not so much to realize the
ideal as to idealize the real*

F. H. Hedge

Lovers, madly attracted to each other, are often incompatible.
Because of their differences in personalities, values, and interests,
they simply cannot live with each other. Although the High-Tech
world can't give us answers to our questions about love and intimacy
or change our incompatibilities, we have more information about
how we as human·beings can live together than we have ever had.
How much of that information you search out and how you apply
that information in your personal life is a matter of individual
choice.

Passion

At least once in your life, you will probably experience a
mad, passionate love affair. In the beginning, you and your lover
can't keep your hands off each other. All your hours are spent
fantasizing about being together. You're obsessed with thoughts of
your lover. And much of your time together is spent making mad,
passionate love. Yet, with time, you learn that passion is a transitory
state.

Passion, in part, is a chemical process. The pleasure centers
in the brain respond to the stimulation of something or someone new. Nature deliberately throws young people into a love
affair to reproduce the race. Yet, human bodies literally cannot
stand passion too long. The chemicals of passion subside to find

a more natural balance.

Passion, in part, is a psychological process. Humans often like the challenge of the new, the exploration of the unknown. Once the danger of the unknown, the excitement of newness and discovery subsides, you are left with the relationship — with the interaction of two persons. Then you see reality.

Some individuals, madly searching for a lasting passion, move from one new lover to another. When ecstasy is gone, they are off on the search for a new partner, leaving behind them a series of broken relationships.

Some of these individuals use sex for self-validation. They need another person to be "wild" about them to prove that they are attractive, desirable, or valuable. They think they are nothing if they do not have a lover. Those who feel compelled to legitimatize their love affairs tally up an impressive number of divorces.

Eventually, most of these searchers learn to find contentment in less passionate marriages based on intimate closeness, stability, and companionship.

Nurturing a Relationship

People who expect relationships to exist forever on a high, passionate, sexual plane will be disappointed. However, it is possible to achieve a balance between familiarity and passion — to create a mixture of security and novelty.

If you want more romance, you must accept the responsibility for putting spark into your permanent relationship. If you want more fun, you can nurture the relationship by being resourceful with how you spend your Prime Time.

Prime Time is the time you concentrate on each other with all your attention. *Other Time* is when you're physically present but your mind is elsewhere; or it's time you spend with necessary activities like washing the car, mowing the lawn, doing the laundry.

When you were courting, most of your Prime Time was spent with each other. Even at work, your attention was not on what you were doing, but on reviewing your time together, looking forward to being together, or planning the next step in your relationship.

But once you begin to live together, you no longer need to make special arrangements to see each other which helps because you can't spend the rest of your life holding hands. Living in the same house includes taking care of the house, food, clothes, and daily living routines.

162

Nurturing romance in a marriage takes deliberate intent. Quality time is important and takes thought and planning. It's not enough simply to be together all the time.

Psychologist Havelock Ellis and his wife lived in separate houses to keep their passion alive. They, in effect, "dated" each other to recreate a series of romantic encounters.

While brief separations work for some couples, most of us do not want Ellis's extreme solution. But you can stay in love with expressions of attention such as gifts, flowers, cards, and phone calls. If you value these things, give them. But do *not* "give" to "get" which is manipulation, not generosity.

If you want to hear authentic loving, caring feelings, say them: "You smell spicy." "You look lovely in that dress." "I feel good when I hold you." Or, if you would feel silly complimenting your mate, you can write "love" letters. Or you can make a date. For example:

"How about meeting me for lunch?"
"When and where?"
"How about tomorrow. I'll pick you up at 1 P.M."

You can arrange a weekend away from home. For example,

"Do you have anything planned for this weekend?"
"Yes, I have a Saturday morning meeting."
"How about the next weekend?"
'That one's free. What do you have in mind?"
*"A mad, passionate love affair with my wife. Meet me at
    the Hilton, Friday night at 6 P.M."*

If you want a secret lover, treat your spouse like one. But don't set up expectations.

These surprises must be for your own enjoyment. You set up a trap for yourself if you expect your partner to "appreciate" your thoughtfulness and return the gifts. If he or she does like what you arrange and follows your lead, that's the frosting on the cake. But great expectations of gratitude often end in disappointment. Whenever you experience disappointment, the problem often lies in your expectations.

You can*not* change your partner. You cannot make another person think, feel, or behave in ways that suit your desires. If you want excitement in your marriage, you will fit your behavior to your partner's comfort level. You will be sensitive to his or her needs.

163

Your reward for the thought and energy you put into your relationship is your own enjoyment.

If you like variety, you can experiment with new topics of conversation, new activities, new sex. But be gentle and sensitive – step lightly so as not to offend. If your attempts to put spice into your marriage are manipulative, intended to change your spouse, they won't work.

Checking for Prime Time
1. When did you go out for a romantic dinner?
2. How often do you go out to a movie or play?
3. Did you go dancing when dating? How long since you have gone dancing? Would you like to go dancing?
4. When was the last time you went on a picnic or to the beach?
5. How often do you plan to do something together that is fun?
6. Do you spend most weekends working on your car, house, laundry, or household chores?
7. How long since you bought your mate a surprise gift?
8. How long since you have explored some new place or activity together?
9. How long since you went away for a weekend alone together?
10. Do you still have meaningful conversations about yourselves, your relationship, your dreams, your personal aspirations?

However – a word of warning. We tend to be idealistic and imagine that we can please each other just because we have good intentions. "The road to hell is paved with good intentions." Don't set yourself up for a disappointment. Disappointment tells you that your expectations are unrealistic.

Many of us get involved in work, social activities, friends, and family. By inattention, we allow our marriage to go stale or get boring. What is considered boring by one person is comfort to another.

You can also allow your relationship to follow its own course. Sometimes focusing or paying too much attention can be like an irritation to the more independent person. If your partner is comfortable with the status quo, perhaps nothing needs to be changed.

You can put the spark back into your marriages by yourself.

164

Make a commitment to keep your marriage alive and vibrant. You can bring new friends into your marriage. You can experiment with new experiences and interests. Travel to new places. Surprise can spark renewed feelings of love or discomfort with the unexpected. Sensitivity to your partner's comfort levels will be rewarded.

Checking Out Assumptions

We often think we know what pleases our partner, or worse, we believe our partner knows what pleases us. These assumptions need to be checked, validated through communicating. When actions indicate dissatisfaction, you can ask, "Are you feeling uncomfortable. . .?" "What would you like. . . ?"

However, an insecure person who constantly questions the emotional state of the other can make a relationship worse. In a strong marriage, spouses are willing to confront each other with honest feedback. "I enjoyed that. . . ." "I don't feel good about that. . . ." "I feel uncomfortable when you do that. . . ." "I feel excited when you do that. . . ." "I appreciate you for. . . ."

If you communicate because you want your partner to do the same, that could be manipulative. You can ask for more communication, but you can't make someone share or explore their feelings to satisfy you.

The major tasks in a marriage are to satisfy the self, to challenge the self, to nurture the self. Ultimately, if each of us took care of the self, the marriage would be in great shape.

A loving relationship survives best in an atmosphere of freedom where two independent individuals cooperate to create a satisfying relationship which includes boring times, satisfying times, and exciting moments; swings in moods from upsets to comfort, to intense highs.

It is important to retain your individuality. Although you have some common interests, you also have some separate interests. If you are insecure, you may feel that you must be with your partner constantly. Fear of separation may also be a fear that one of you will be attracted to another person.

In some marriages where the partners enjoy different activities, some couples are willing to allow each person to satisfy his own choices. For example, one will go to Hawaii while the other goes hunting. One reward of a separation is the excitement you experience when you are together again.

Although you enjoy some interests in common, you can also arrange to satisfy your separate preferences. You might find you

165

have the capacity to go some places alone and enjoy yourself. Or you can find a friend who enjoys what you like to accompany you which allows your spouse to satisfy his or her own preferences.

Human relationships are, by nature, cyclical. You can learn that when the relationship seems "down," it will soon move up. Also when it is "high," it will then move down. Excitement and intensity in a relationship ebb and flow.

Just when you think the passion and lust have gone out of your marriage, something will happen. He or she will touch you, gaze into your eyes, and it will flare up. Just when you think the spark has died, it will surprise you one more time. Through such cycles, you may find that love lasts forever.

What Makes a Marriage Last?

The average duration of a marriage in the United States is 9.4 years. Although it may seem, at times, that no one is happily married, researchers have surveyed married couples and found many of them feel that they are happy.

In June, 1986, *Psychology Today* published an article on marriage. Of 351 couples, both husband and wife in 19 marriages said they were unhappily married but staying together for a variety of reasons; in 32 marriages, only one partner said he or she was unhappy. *Three hundred couples said they were happily married.*

Although each husband and wife responded individually to the questionnaire, the top reasons they gave for their lasting marriages were almost identical.

These are the top seven reasons in order of frequency:

1. My spouse is my best friend.
2. I like my spouse as a person.
3. Marriage is a long-term commitment.
4. Marriage is sacred.
5. We agree on aims and goals.
6. My spouse has grown more interesting.
7. I want the relationship to succeed.

Other reasons which varied lightly between men and women in order of frequency included:

* We laugh together.
* We agree on a philosophy of life.
* We agree on how and how often to show affection.

166

- We agree about our sex life.
- I confide in my spouse.
- We share outside hobbies and interests.
- We have a stimulating exchange of ideas.
- I am proud of my spouse's achievements.
- An enduring marriage is important to social stability.

Many happily married people said that over time their mates became more interesting to them. One man said, "I have watched her grow and have shared with her both the pain and the exhilaration of her journey."

Less Than Perfect

Although these individuals were aware of each other's flaws, they didn't dwell on them. They acknowledged rough times in their marriage. Even in a loving relationship, they knew that, at times, they would be angry, upset, or miserable. But they found personality qualities in their mates that made these times tolerable; such qualities as caring, empathy, and integrity.

These individuals did not create drama or upsets. They avoided making their partners wrong or denying them love. They trusted each other not to deliberately dig at each other's weaknesses or wounds.

The individuals in these happy marriages were concerned about each other. They believed that marriage sometimes required them to grit their teeth and plunge ahead in spite of problems. One man said, "Commitment means a willingness to be unhappy for a while. . . . You're not going to be happy with each other all the time."

Couples who stay together share attitudes toward their spouses and share marriage values. They also agree about aims and goals in life. They agreed that a sense of humor is valuable.

One surprising result was fewer than ten percent of them thought sex could keep a marriage together. Yet they were satisfied with their sexual relations. While some reported a diminishing sex life, a few indicated improvement over time. Generally, they were satisfied with less-than-ideal sex. Many agreed they would rather be married to their spouse with less-than-ideal sex life than be married to someone else even with a better sex life.

These individuals expressed a willingness to have some conflicts in their marriages. They did not expect perfection all the time. Yet no one mentioned self-denial to please a spouse as a solution to conflict.

They were willing to discuss problems and negotiate disagree-

167

ments. They dealt with each crisis as a challenge, an opportunity to let go of separateness and move into a more intimate experience of married love. They viewed their marriages as sitting on a scale where give and take balanced.

Happily married couples like each other. They are friends. They share attitudes, values, and behavioral patterns which contribute to enduring relationships. Leo Tolstoy wrote, "Happy families are all alike." Readers can use this study as a model of values, attitudes, and beliefs that result in a lasting, happy marriage.

Pat is my best friend

Married Love

During the sexual revolution of the '60's, sex became a media event. Books and magazine articles stressed sex as a counting game: how many times, how many different techniques, how many different partners, how many minutes in duration. The performance mystique offered visions of eroticism and the exotic.

Readers became very insecure as they compared themselves with these ideals espoused by sex experts. Many people felt compelled to try all kinds of strange sexual activities. If a woman was not multi-orgasmic, she felt something was wrong with her. If a man couldn't hold an erection for hours, he felt he couldn't measure up. After a decade of this kind of exploration and experimentation – influenced by the experts who told people how they were *supposed to be*, the values changed again.

The sexual revolution slayed some old Victorian dragons, but it created new ones with its subtle but pervasive prescriptions. Recreational sex, divorced from love and creation, lacked empathy, compassion, morality and responsibility. After the newness wore off, it was dull. Individuals felt depersonalized and devalued. Loveless sex was, for most people, impossible.

Even though love is threatening because it involves risks – the possibility of pain, rejection, or failure – the quest of a long-term relationship in which both partners voluntarily commit themselves to exclusivity is what most people want. Monogamy is again an important value.

Some of the virtues required for monogamy to be satisfying are enthusiasm, loyalty, courtesy and patience. Mutual interests and a shared common vision of life's purpose also help. The ability to support each other emotionally, not only in good times but when life doesn't seem to be working, is essential.

Married people learn that what a marriage needs is intimacy and closeness rather than physical orgasms. What they find out is that they really want cozy sex. A comfortable snuggle is, in its own way, more satisfying. Familiar love is cuddling, warmth, private time together in loving renewal of commitments.

Drifting off to sleep with a married partner of many years can't be compared with the first year. Sexual love and sexual needs change during marriage. Romance in the later years is different.

As we look back at the beginning, many of us tend to idealize the past. We block out the early embarrassments; shame that our bodies aren't perfect, embarrassment about sharing a bathroom, fear that one of us will snore. Expecting daily marriage to imitate the beginning period is like drinking champagne every night from the same glass. It gets mechanical.

Sex is an expression of your personalities and your relationship. It doesn't have to meet any outside standards — especially those written by The Experts in Women's Magazines. Stop comparing yourself to others, to another time, to another mate. Set your own norms. Then expect them to change.

Sex can be as simple as kissing, hugging, and falling asleep holding hands. Being held, stroked, petted regularly satisfies most individuals. Again, however, some individuals need less physical contact than others. The amount of physical contact is not necessarily correlated with commitment and loyalty. If there is a great discrepancy between the amount of physical contact two individuals want in a marriage, once recognized and discussed, some kinds of accommodation are required for the marriage to continue.

More important than physical sex is trust, knowing you can bare your thoughts and your vulnerabilities to a partner who will honor them. In familiar intimacy, you know you are really loved for who you are, not for some fantasy you can't live up to. Familiar intimacy is relaxed, deeply fulfilling in the secure knowledge that you are truly loved for yourself.

Marital Skills

A couple's ability to talk over problems effectively is more crucial to compatibility than even how much a couple thinks they are in love. It is how you deal with your incompatibilities that is most important.

Happily married couples develop a "private language," a set of subtle cues and private words that have special meanings. They understand exactly what their spouses mean. They show a high degree of responsiveness to each other in sharing events of the day. The absence of such responsiveness leads to tensions. After years of sharing, with interest, each other's daily histories, no one outside the marriage has as much background information. We want to be known. We want our lives to be shared.

In general, women are more comfortable with confrontation. But both husbands and wives can learn to switch to conciliation in the heat of an argument. Although men tend to withdraw and women tend to argue, in a happy marriage, couples seem able to prevent an escalation. Those couples who communicate well can best prevent emotional injury.

Occasional tensions are inevitable in any marriage. The desire for intimacy and the need for self-identity as a separate person exist in a state of tension. Marriage is a forum for the negotiation of a balance between these conflicting urges.

One paradox is that as a couple's intimacy increases, you often see a corresponding increase in their desire for distance. How satisfied they are depends to a large extent on how they communicate these needs.

Important communication skills that you can develop include the following:

- Focus on one issue at a time.
- Make other preoccupations clear. ("I had a bad day at work.")
- Stop the action when repetitive cycles of conflict begin.
- Be specific in criticizing. For each criticism, add a specific example of praise. (When I see your jacket on the floor, I feel taken advantage of. And I appreciate it when you hang up your pajamas.)
- Edit what you say to avoid emotional injury. It is unproductive to dredge up past events or old grudges.

When you empower your partner, your relationship gets stronger. When you exude a positive attitude, everyone and everything around you is made better by your presence.

Empowering Your Partner

No one is so secure that he or she never has doubts about self-value. You can enrich your marriage by reenforcing your partner's self-esteem, by reminding him or her of strengths. Learn to communicate your positive thoughts and attitudes. Here are some statements that might be useful:

170

- You can do it, and I will assist you if you want me to.
- I love you.
- I value you.
- I will stand behind you.
- How can I enrich your life?"
- We can have what we want from life.
- Our life together is great.

Marriages thrive on how well a couple communicates support for each other.

Commitment

In a committed, supportive relationship, each person is valued and each person's life is the prime consideration. A good relationship is alive with mutual support.

A good relationship is *not* safe or certain or perfect. Commitment is an act of courage. Your relationship will work because you are responsible and committed. It is commitment from both of you that allows you to have intensity and aliveness in your relationship. When you give yourself, you receive. You get what you want.

A commonly mistaken fantasy is, "If only I could find the right person, marriage would be beautiful." The truth is *YOU MUST BE THE RIGHT PERSON.* If you are not right for marriage, marriage will not fulfill you.

The commitment you have to producing the kind of relationship you want builds the momentum that enables you to operate at levels where you give and get back more than you have put in. Commitment says, "You can count on me." If you want commitment, give it.

Freedom and intimacy are to a person what sun and water are to a plant: both must be present at the same time for a marriage to flourish. In an evolving relationship, spouses engage in a process that encourages individuality while increasing intimacy.

Partners in a permanent relationship weave in and out of deep connection. You cannot always be intimate. But once you have been, you know how to recreate the same connection.

Each of you encourages the other to express and understand the self on ever-deepening levels. Although openly discussing your fears and vulnerabilities seem frightening, it is actually the best way of achieving the security you long for.

Rather than false security based on promises, obligation, or fear; a permanent relationship endures from the matchless value

171

gained from being with another person who wants you to be who you are, wants to be with you, wants to understand you and wants to facilitate your emotional growth. Mutual acceptance and love contribute to satisfaction and happiness.

In the end, most of us choose love, marriage, sex, and parenthood — all of which are quite different now from what they were in the past. As we mature, our ideas about human relationships change.

E. M. Forster wrote,

"The road sometimes doubles, to be sure, but. . .who can doubt that its general tendency is onward? To what goal we know not — it may be to some mountain where we shall touch the sky, it may be over precipices into the sea. But that it goes forward — who can doubt that? It is the thought of that that makes us strive to excel, each in his own way. . . ."

In the context of our changing values, the present bears little resemblance to life in the past. Periodically, each of us must reassess our human relationships — the meaning of love, marriage, sex, parenthood. We are always learning, expanding, developing. We can find our own answers to life. *(and assist each other in "finding answers" by 1) listening empathically; 2) being emotionally supportive; 3) being "enabling" toward partner; 4) complimenting, offering unsolicited positive reinforcement and praise*

172

Suggested Readings

SUGGESTED READINGS

Belliveau, Fred and Richter, Lin. *Understanding Human Sexual Inadequacy*. New York: Bantam, 1979.

Bernard, Jessie. *The Future of Marriage*. New York: World, 1972.

Berne, Eric. *Games People Play*. New York: Grove Press, 1964.

Brazelton, T. Berry. *Working & Caring*. Reading, Mass: Addison Wesley, 1985.

Bry, Adelaine. *Friendship: How to Have a Friend and Be a Friend*. New York: Grosset & Dunlap, 1979.

Bryson, Jeff, & Bryson, Rebecca. *Dual Career Couples*. New York: Human Sciences Press, 1978.

Burger, Hinki Hait. *The Executive Wife*. New York: Collier Books, 1986.

Ellis, Albert and Harper, Robert. *Creative Marriage*. New York: Lyle Stuart, 1961.

Frankl, Viktor. *Man's search for meaning*. New York: Simon & Schuster, 1972.

French, Merilyn. *Beyond Power*. New York: Ballantine Books, 1985.

Friday, Nancy. *My Secret Garden*. New York: Simon & Schuster, 1974.

Gillies, Jerry. *Friends: The Power and Potential of the Company You Keep*. New York: Coward, McCann & Geoghegan, Inc., 1976.

Greenwald, Jerry. *Creative Intimacy: How to break the Patterns that Poison Your Relationships*. New York: Simon & Schuster, 1975.

Hall, Francise & Hall, Douglas. *The Two Career Couple: He Works, She Works, but How Does the Relationship Work?* Menlo Park, California: Addison Wesley Pub., 1979.

Hopson, Barrie & Hopson, Charlotte. *Intimate Feedback: A Lovers*

Guide to Getting in Touch with Each Other. New York: Simon & Schuster, 1973.

Ilich, John & Jones, Barbara. *Successful Negotiating Skills For Women*. Playboy, 1981.

Irish, Richard. *How to Live Separate & Together: A Guide for Working Couples*. New York: Anchor Press, 1981.

James, Muriel and Savary, Louis. *The Heart of Friendship*. New York: Harper & Row, 1978.

Keys, Margaret Frings. *Staying Married*. Millbrae, California: Les Femmes, 1975.

Kimball, Bayle. *The 50-50 Marriage*. Boston: Beacon Press, 1983.

Kozmetsky, Ronya & George. *Making It Together: A Survival Manual for the Executive Family*. New York: Free Press, 1981.

Krantzler, Mel. *Creative Marriage*. New York: McGraw Hill Books, Inc., 1981.

Lazarus, Arnold. *Marital Myths*. San Luis Obispo, California: Impact Pub., 1985.

Ledere, William J. and Jackson, Don D. *The Mirages of Marriage*. New York: Norton Company, Inc., 1968.

Luthman, Shirley Gerke, with Kirschenbaum, Martin. *The Dynamic Family*. Palo Alto, California: Science and Behavioral Books, 1974.

Masters, William H. and Johnson, Virginia E. *The Pleasure Bond*. Boston: Little, Brown & Co., 1970.

Miller, Sherod, Nunnaly, Elam W., and Wackman, Daniel, B. *Alive and Aware: Improving Communication in Relationships*. Minneapolis, Minnesota: International Communication Programs, Inc., 1975.

Nierenberg, Gerald I. *The Art of Negotiating*. New York: Cornerstone Library, 1968.

Mornell, Pierre. *Passive Men, Wild Women*. New York: Ballantine Books, 1979.

Norwood, Robin. *Women Who Love Too Much*. New York: Pocket Books, 1985.

Penqelley, Eric T. *Sex and Human Life*. Maine: Addison Wesley Pub. Co., 1974.

Porat, Frieda, *Changing Your Life Style*. Secaucus, New Jersey: Lyle Stuart, Inc., 1973.

Porat, Frieda. *Positive Selfishness: A Practical Guide to Self Esteem*. Millbrae, California: Celestial Arts, 1977.

Porat, Frieda. *How To Be Your Own Marriage Counselor*. New York: Rawson Associates, 1978.

Porat, Frieda. *Creative Procrastination: Organizing Your Own Life.*

San Francisco: Harper & Row, 1980.

Putney, Snell and Putney, Gail. *The Adjusted American*. New York: Harper Colophon, 1966.

Rand, Ayn. *The Virtue of Selfishness: A New Concept of Egoism*. New York: New American Library, 1964.

Richardson, Jerry & Margolis, Joel. *The Magic of Rapport*. San Francisco: Harbor Publications, 1981.

Satir, Virginia. *People Making*. Palo Alto, California: Science & Behavior Books, 1972.

Siegel, Gorelick, B. *The Working Parents' Guide to Child Care*. New York: Little Brown & Co., 1983.

Smith, Gerald. *Me & You & Us*. New York: Peter, H. Wyden, 1971.

Shostrom, Everett L., and Kavanaugh, James. *Between Man & Woman*. New York: Bantam Books, 1972.

Walker, Glynnis. *Second Wife, Second Best: Managing Your Marriage as a Second Wife*. Garden City, New York: Doubleday, 1984.

Wandervelde, Maryanne. *The Changing Life of the Corporate Wife*. New York: Warner Books, 1979.

Wandere, Zev, and Fabian, Erika. *Making Love Work*. New York: Ballentine Books, 1979.

Winfield, Fairlee, E. *Commuter Marriage: Living Together Apart*. New York: Columbia University, 1985.

Winter, Gibson, *Love & Conflict*. New York: Doubelday & Co., 1961.

Weitzman, Lenore. *The Marriage Contract: A Guide to Living with Lovers & Spouses*. New York; The Free Press, 1981.